MW01122018

DA

Rune Arlidge

Rune Arlidge

Michael Healey

Playwrights Canada Press
Toronto • Canada

Playwrights Canada Press
215 Spadina Avenue, Suite 230, Toronto, Ontario CANADA M5T 2C7
416-703-0013
orders@playwrightscanada.com • www.playwrightscanada.com

Playwrights Canada Press acknowledges the support of
the taxpayers of Canada and the province of Ontario through
The Canada Council for the Arts and the Ontario Arts Council.

Cover photo of Jane Spidell by Cylla von Tiedeman.
Cover design & production editing: JLArt

Library and Archives Canada Cataloguing in Publication

Healey, Michael
    Rune Arlidge / Michael Healey.

A play.
ISBN 0-88754-732-X

    I. Title.

PS8565.E14R85 2004   C812'.54   C2004-903429-4

First edition: July 2004.
Printed and bound by AGMV at Quebec, Canada.

This play was written for Jane Spidell and Ari Cohen.

Rune Arlidge premiered at Tarragon Theatre, Toronto, in March 2004 with the following company:

Fiona Reid	Frances
John Dolan	Tom, Tom Junior
Jane Spidell	Rune Arlidge
Julie Stewart	Michelle
Rick Roberts	Matthew
Ari Cohen	Harvar
Severn Thompson	Lillian

Directed by Leah Cherniak
Stage Managed by Arwen MacDonell
Set and Costumes designed by Charlotte Dean
Lights designed by Andrea Lundy
Sound design by Kirk Elliot

—•— Playwright's Acknowledgements —•—

Rune Arlidge received workshops at the Tarragon Theatre in 2002, and at the Shaw Festival in 2002 and 2003. My thanks to both companies, and to the actors who read those drafts.

Ari Cohen wrote the fat-in-your-new-pants line, and I remain eternally in his debt.

—•— Characters —•—

Act One: A cottage, 1994

Rune Arlidge, 20
Michelle, her sister, 26
Frances, her mother, 58
Matthew, her boyfriend, 23
Tom, the handyman, 59

Act Two: The same, ten years later

Harvar, 38
Lillian, almost 10

Act Three: The same, fifteen years later

Tom Junior, 50

Tom and Tom Junior are played by the same actor

—•— Note —•—

Because playgoers can't be counted on to look at their programmes, we decided in the first production to include briefly projected slides at the top of each act. They read:

August, 1994;
Ten years later;
and
Fifteen years later.

Act One

The porch of a cottage in southern Ontario. 1994. Late summer.
Dawn. We hear TOM's truck pull up, the door open and shut.
TOM enters, and bangs on the cottage door. Eventually, FRANCES
comes to the screen.

TOM
Morning.

FRANCES
Is that Tom?

TOM
Missus Arlidge, you can see it's me.

FRANCES
What are you accusing me of? I can't see it's you. Not necessarily.
You're backlit.

TOM
It's Tom.

FRANCES
And also, there's the filthy screen between us. So maybe I can't see
it's you. Maybe you're just some shapeless grey hulk, there on the
other side of this not particularly useful door, this filthy door.
I mean why does everyone–

RUNE
(from within) Mother, shut up.

FRANCES
–everyone is so ready to accuse me of something. Do you know how
early it is? I was seconds ago asleep just over there, and now I'm
standing here, and I don't even remember how I got here.

TOM
Missus Arlidge, it's Tom. Sorry. I'm here–

FRANCES
I can't see anything. I can't see anything. What time is it?

RUNE

(*from within*) Mother, shut up.

FRANCES

Good Lord, it's – what time does that say? I will not shut up. We're being accosted probably. It's – what?

TOM

It's early.

FRANCES

Good Lord. What does that – is that six o'clock?

TOM

Rune said I should–

FRANCES

Tom––if that's who it is––no offense now, but, are you out of your mind?

TOM

Rune said–

FRANCES

Why on earth would you come out here and knock at this time of the morning? You can't be Tom. He wouldn't do this. Tom Ilesic is a sweet man. A helpful and useful–

MICHELLE

(*from a different part of the cottage*) Mother, SHUT THE FUCK UP.

FRANCES

Yes, very nice, that's fine, sorry to disturb you ladies, but a man has come to rape and kill us all.

RUNE

(*appearing behind her mother*) In which order.

TOM

I could come back.

RUNE

Hi, Mr. Ilesic. No. Come on in. Move it, mother.

FRANCES

Wait! How do you know it's–

> RUNE *has opened the door, and steps outside. She is in her pyjamas, as is her mother. And when MICHELLE emerges, she'll be in pyjamas, too.*

Oh. Hello, Tom.

TOM

Missus Arlidge. Hey Rune.

RUNE

Thanks for coming.

TOM

It's okay.

FRANCES

Hello, Tom. Why is Tom here?

RUNE

I called Mr. Ilesic to come and fix the water.

FRANCES

Yes. What's the matter with the water?

RUNE

Nothing. The water's perfect. It just doesn't come out of anything.

FRANCES

Oh, the pump. Your fucking father–. Tom, would you like some coffee?

TOM

Sure.

FRANCES

God. Me too.

> *FRANCES steps onto the porch, throws herself into a chair. TOM heads inside. A pause.*

(of the landscape) Pretty.

> *A pause.*

Michelle!

MICHELLE

(from within) Mother?

FRANCES

Get up and make some coffee. *(to RUNE)* How are you, um, feeling today?

> *A pause.*

You and your sister have to race today. Don't forget.

RUNE

The race is today?

FRANCES

Nobody in this family listens. Yes. Today. One o'clock or something. It's on the thing.

RUNE

I'm not going today. I have to stay here.

FRANCES

Don't even start.

RUNE

I'm not going anywhere. I have to stay here.

FRANCES

You have to–. Now listen. There are a dozen pennants in there. Hanging proudly in there, singles, and doubles and under 13s and father-daughter things, and whatnot, in there. You and your sister and your father earned every one of them. It's one of the only joys of my summer, watching for you to return with another pennant. It's one of the few things that makes this place tolerable, mainly because it meant that the summer was almost over. And there is a four-year gap now, in there, a four-year pennant gap. And I do not judge, I mean, of course you would go to school, and your sister had, all the things to do she did, and other sometime family members developed other, obscure priorities unrelated to those parental and matrimonial ones he had already fucking acquired–

RUNE

How do you speak in paragraphs? It's barely light out.

FRANCES

Never mind me. Never mind attacking my syntax. Today is the day the pennant drought ends for this family. End of story.

RUNE

No. I'm…. No.

FRANCES

I'll get a shoehorn, we'll fit it into your incredible schedule. Between the sleeping 20 hours a day and the staring at the inside of the refrigerator.

> *MICHELLE comes out carrying a bottle of red wine, a corkscrew and a tumbler.*

Good morning. Don't make any plans for later. You and your sister are paddling.

MICHELLE

Anybody I know?

FRANCES
You're going to win another pennant for your mother.

MICHELLE
Oh. Okay.

FRANCES
Really?

MICHELLE
Why not? My stroke isn't what it was, but I'm sure I'll– *(struggling with the cork)* motherfucking – what time is this?

FRANCES
One o'clock. So you'll do it?

MICHELLE
Sure. If I'm conscious. Why not. C'mon, you stupid–. Is it at the thing?

FRANCES
See, Rune? Your sister, who's normally the cunt about these things, is willing to paddle for me.

RUNE
I don't want to.

FRANCES
Frankly, young lady, what you want is of no concern to– *(noticing MICHELLE and the wine)* what in the hell are you doing?

MICHELLE
(the bottle between her legs) Motherfucking Niagara piece of–.

FRANCES
I believe I asked for coffee.

MICHELLE
Can't – make – coffee.

> *TOM comes outside.*

TOM
It's the pump.

FRANCES
Is it the pump? That comes as absolutely no surprise to me.

TOM
Have to go down below.

MICHELLE
Mr. Ilesic? Can you get that?

TOM
Sure.

TOM takes the bottle, pulls on the corkscrew.

Boy. That's in there, eh? You know, if you store this on its side, the cork won't dry out.

FRANCES
Now what am I being accused of? Improper wine storage? That's the limit. For your information, that bottle of wine was never meant to be drunk. It was brought here by some guests, many years ago, and I left it prominently displayed as an example of an unacceptable bottle of wine to bring to someone's cottage.

The fact that this one has decided to open it at this disgustingly early hour and disgustingly late date means I now have to take advice about how to keep wine, from a man, a nice man, to be sure, but a man who nonetheless drives to *Penetanguishene* for a cosmopolitan experience. Which is beyond the limit. You're a nice man, Tom. But, I mean, come on.

TOM
No, I understand.

TOM has opened the bottle, and he hands it to MICHELLE. He then steps off the porch and removes some of the lattice fronting the crawlspace below. He crawls under the porch with a flashlight and tools. MICHELLE drinks the wine: a quick first glass and then nurses the refill.

FRANCES
(She's looking out over the lake.) It's what time of the day, and I've already reached the limit. Did your father ever teach you to fish?

RUNE
No.

MICHELLE
Yes.

FRANCES
That's nice. Did you enjoy it?

MICHELLE
No.

RUNE
Yes.

A pause.

FRANCES
Did I ever tell you the story of how your father and I found this place?

MICHELLE and RUNE immediately rise and disappear inside.

FRANCES
We found it in a canoe. We had a cabin rented across the lake, that little place that called itself a resort. We howled with laughter at that, when we pulled up. A half-dozen shacks on the water and a couple of leaky canoes. Howled with laughter. Of course, a couple of nights there and it stopped being funny. After one night in the bed, your father woke with a red lump on his stomach, which we later learned was where the spider had chosen to burrow in to lay her eggs. It was two weeks later, and he was at his doctor, who told him he had inadvertently become a spider egg host. The doctor had him look away while he lanced the bump, but your father glanced back in time to see all the baby spiders spill out of his skin.

But oh, God, the sex. That cabin, for that week, 1960-something; probably only because there was no television. There were no televised sports. Which, incidentally, is how you got your name. His love of televised sports. Did you know that?

So, one day we took a canoe and paddled out onto the lake, and sort of got drifted all the way across here, and your father shouted and swore at me, but a blister's a blister and so that was the paddling over, as far as I was concerned. Drifting. The view was wonderful, all that green and all that blue, the sun getting lower; your father screaming behind me.

We wound up here, in this bay, and this place had a for sale sign on it and we argued about whether or not he should break in here and use the phone to call someone from the resort to come and pick us up. He was standing down there, in the water, up to his ankles, holding the canoe, and when he finally stepped out of the water to do what I'd told him, he saw the leeches. He had cut his foot on one of the sharp stones in our bay and they had just come running for him. And when he fainted, he was just like one of those inflated dolls you punch: he hit the dock with his head, and sprung right back up into place. He broke that window and found a box of salt and took care of the leeches. And he was so embarrassed at the mess he made, he put in an offer on the place, just to be polite. It was absurdly low. It took them forty minutes to accept.

A pause.

FRANCES
All the absent men.

A pause. TOM backs out of the crawlspace.

Why, here's one now. Tom. Tell me something.

TOM
Any idea what this is?

FRANCES
Let me see?

He brings it to her. It's a piece of wadded-up tinfoil.

Well, I suspect you'd have to ask Rune. She was down there last. She's convinced she knows how to fix the pump because her father dragged her under there once and showed her what to do. Except as we know, he was really quite clueless when it came to the plumbing. In fact, he was worse than that: he was clueless and deluded. About plumbing. Anybody's plumbing. If you take my meaning. Would you like some coffee?

TOM
Not falling for that one again.

FRANCES
No, I'll get one of the girls to boil some water from the lake.

TOM
No thanks. I gotta go. Thomas Junior and I are putting up the new place across the way. He'll be waiting. Tell Rune she had the right idea with this, but that it's gonna take an actual part at this point. I'll pick it up at the end of the day and put it in tomorrow morning.

FRANCES
Same time?

TOM
Fraid so. But at least you'll only have to go a day without.

FRANCES
Hmm. Tell me something.

TOM
All right.

FRANCES

You left the Missus, correct.

TOM

(who is too old to be embarrassed by the likes of her) Correct.

FRANCES

After how many years?

TOM

Moved out two days before the thirty-first anniversary. It was pointed out to me. Several times.

FRANCES

And, if I'm not, could you tell me why?

TOM

Well, Frances, I guess I don't know exactly. I just, I don't really know. It was a long time to be married.

FRANCES

That must have been incredibly difficult for her. There not being a reason.

TOM

I guess so.

FRANCES

Yes.

TOM

Did Mister Arlidge have a reason?

FRANCES

Not as such. No serious reason.

TOM

Huh. Men.

A beat.

Girls all right?

FRANCES

Hmm? Yes, thanks. Far as I can tell.

TOM

That's good.

FRANCES

They hate me.

TOM

No.

FRANCES

Genuinely. I pretend it rankles. Do you love your children?

TOM

Just got the one. And he's no child these days. I can just about stand his company all day long if there's something to busy us, like this monster cottage.

FRANCES

Yes.

TOM

Yesterday we put in the hot tub. Today it's a freestanding sauna combination goddamn smokehouse. So this guy can spend his summers making his own bacon. And sweating.

A pause.

Maybe I can come back some evening, play some cards.

FRANCES

Oh. Tom. Oh. You're not my type at all.

TOM

Jesus, lady, you think you're mine?

FRANCES

Well.

A pause.

God. It never, ever gets any easier, does it.

TOM

I guess not.

A pause.

Okay.

FRANCES

Yes.

TOM

See you in the morning.

FRANCES

Yes.

He exits. The truck starts, and leaves. MICHELLE comes out of the cottage with the bottle, the glass and a roll of toilet paper. She puts down the bottle, takes the last slug out of the glass, and puts it down. As she disappears around the side of the cottage:

FRANCES
Yes, sorry. Just 'til tomorrow.

A beat. RUNE comes out.

(handing her the tinfoil) Tom says nice try, but unfortunately you've inherited your father's delusional plumbing condition.

RUNE
Why'd you scare him off?

FRANCES
Good Lord. I didn't scare anyone off. That was flirting.

RUNE
That was flirting? Jesus Christ. One of us has no idea what the hell they're doing.

FRANCES
That's right dear. How is your fellow. What was his name?

RUNE
Matt.

FRANCES
That's right. How is he?

RUNE
He's fine.

FRANCES
I see. Do you want to tell me about it, dear?

RUNE
I don't think so.

FRANCES
Thank God. Did you make some coffee?

RUNE
No, Mother, I didn't.

FRANCES
Do you not know how?

RUNE
I don't want any.

FRANCES
Oh, you don't. Don't you. Well, young lady, the question of your needs, what you want any of or not want, is not the issue here. Perhaps this is the root of your problem with this fellow. Not being able to appreciate the needs of others because of the apparent enormity of your own is a big problem. It's crippling. It's fundamentally a lack of empathy. Which is the glue of the world, my dear. The glue of the world.

RUNE
No, I'll tell you what my problem is–

FRANCES
Your problem, if I may, is that you haven't made *any frigging coffee.* You know, I blame myself. An ability to empathise is probably a mother's job to impart. Another in the long list of failures. I tried with you girls, I really did, but somehow, I was always trying at the wrong thing.

　　MICHELLE enters, smoking a joint. To RUNE:

MICHELLE
Want some of that?

RUNE
Not really.

　　RUNE takes the joint.

FRANCES
Once I spent God knows how long making you a motherfucking fly-ing saucer suit, don't ask me why, school probably, all I knew was here was my chance to behave in a motherly fashion. And I gave it everything. You have no idea. Nights, sitting up, developing new ways to attach tinfoil to cardboard so it wouldn't fall off. Tinfoil attachment methods Dupont would take years and billions to develop. Until your father pointed out no one had eaten a decent meal for weeks. The house was a wreck. You children were filthy.

MICHELLE
So? Is he coming up today?

RUNE
No.

FRANCES
God only knows what I looked like. And it was that moment the real estate agent began bringing young couples through the house.

MICHELLE
Why not?

FRANCES
Your father had neglected to mention we were selling the house.

RUNE
I don't know. But it was yesterday.

MICHELLE
He was supposed to come up yesterday?

RUNE
That's what we said.

FRANCES
One of you, I forget which, actually came down with actual scurvy. From all the poor nutrition. First case in two hundred years, they said. What?

RUNE
I can't say I'm sorry, actually.

MICHELLE
Why.

FRANCES
What?

RUNE
He's been very weird lately. I think he's trying to figure out how to dump me. He's being nice.

MICHELLE
He is nice. He's big and nice.

FRANCES
You've invited people out here?

RUNE
No, he's *being* nice.

MICHELLE
He's too nice, if you ask me.

FRANCES
Have you invited people out here?

MICHELLE
And probably too big.

RUNE
He's being shifty and secretive and *nice*. He wants to make sure I see his carefully concealed agony.

FRANCES
Unbelievable. What are these people supposed to eat?

RUNE
I'm supposed to appreciate his bravery during this very difficult period of his trying to figure out how to dump me.

MICHELLE
Are you sure that's what he's doing ?

RUNE
Of course not. I get to guess.

FRANCES
Honest to God.

RUNE
But his not showing up at all is a pretty solid indicator, I think.

FRANCES
I thought we had agreed that this–

MICHELLE
Mother, you can stay, but you've *got* to shut the fuck up.

A pause. FRANCES stands, and goes indoors. MICHELLE and RUNE look at each other. Eventually, from inside:

FRANCES
You people don't treat me properly.

MICHELLE
Yeah, well...

RUNE looks at her.

All right. I'm sorry. I'll come in in a second and poach some eggs.

FRANCES
(at the screen) If you want. Don't make one for me, though. Your poached eggs are dreadful. They're all over the place. Your poached eggs can't concentrate. I'm going back to bed.

MICHELLE
Capital idea. But go to bed. Don't just fall asleep on the couch again.

FRANCES

I find that bed slightly nauseating, I don't know why. Oh, yes. Your father slept in it.

MICHELLE

Go sleep in mine, then.

FRANCES

Yes. That's bound to be a much more wholesome experience. All right, then. Good night.

A pause. RUNE gets up and looks inside. She nods to MICHELLE; the coast is clear.

MICHELLE

Is she worse, lately?

RUNE

That's a really interesting question. We should examine that.

MICHELLE

Yeah, let's get right on that.

RUNE

Yeah.

A pause.

MICHELLE

Did I tell you?

RUNE

What.

MICHELLE

I got offered a job the other day. I forgot if I told you that.

RUNE

No you didn't. Like a real job?

MICHELLE

Oh, fuck, no. Bobby, that, you know, guy? From the gas station bathroom? Calls up and asks if I want to be the *sous chef* in his new restaurant.

RUNE

What's a *sous chef*?

MICHELLE

No idea. I ask him if he knows I've never cooked anything in my life. Says he doesn't care. Asks if he can come over and talk about it.

I more or less say no. While he's on his way, I figure out he's married. Which he at first denies.

RUNE
You're getting better.

MICHELLE
Yes I am. I can spot 'em a mile off, me. Anyway, we're having sex, which is kind of weird because his penis has a definite curve to the left.

RUNE
Really.

MICHELLE
Really. It's like he was constantly nudging me over toward the door. Like he was trying very subtly to get me out of the room.

RUNE
His left or your left?

MICHELLE
Well, darling, it depends which way I'm facing, doesn't it? At the end, I told him that based on his technique as a lover, I didn't think I'd want to ever eat at his restaurant. And so I wouldn't want to work there, either.

RUNE
You total bitch.

MICHELLE
I was trying. But he said he found my comments interesting. Said I had a head for marketing. Completely impervious to insult. In some ways, the perfect man. Well, no, you've got the perfect man.

RUNE
Christ. You think so?

MICHELLE
I suppose. If he dumps you, then he will absolutely become the perfect man. He will in retrospect become the perfect, mysterious guy who you let get away. It's how these things work. If he doesn't dump you, then you have God knows how long to figure out he's not the guy you thought he was. Time plus proximity equals, well, grossness. Time plus separation equals, uh, the opposite of grossness; whatever, you know, whatever that is. And if I'm going to continue to dispense wisdom, I need another fucking drink.

RUNE
Are you okay?

MICHELLE
I'm smashing, pumpkin. Why do you ask?

RUNE
Well, because in spite of its variety, your diet lately would seem to lack balance.

MICHELLE
That kind of thinking is at least ten years out of date. Nobody eats anymore. Nobody fucking eats.

RUNE
And are you, apart from the self-medicating, taking the actual prescribed stuff on a regular basis?

MICHELLE
Oh, sure. More or less. But the regimen is a little unrealistic. I mean, take one when you get up in the morning, take one when you go to bed, who has that rigid a schedule?

RUNE
Yes.

MICHELLE
For a while I tried to tie it into my peeing schedule, but then I found myself taking nine or ten a day. So far, I haven't been able to find anything I do consistently twice daily that I can use to remember to take the friggin' pills.

RUNE
What about fucking strange men?

MICHELLE
Hmm. You may have something there. So, you expect him later? The boy?

RUNE
I don't know. I have no idea what's in his head. I'm amazed I care at all.

MICHELLE
Well don't worry. It won't last. *(rising)* You want a beer?

RUNE
No. I'm gonna go for a swim before the perv with the telescope gets up.

MICHELLE
Oh yes, him. I've been meaning to introduce myself.

RUNE
Have you seen my shoes?

MICHELLE
No. Use mine.

> *MICHELLE goes indoors. RUNE picks up a pair of rotting running shoes nearby. She then goes around the side of the cottage, takes a towel off the line, and heads for the dock. After a beat, FRANCES emerges, still in what she wore to bed, with a plate of toast. She sits. A splash is heard.*

FRANCES
(to the swimming RUNE) Are you out there by yourself? Do you have your shoes on? Eh? Which one of you is that?!?

MICHELLE
(from within) It's her. Stop shouting, for God's sake.

FRANCES
It's her. I see. She's out there by herself, you know.

> *A pause.*

You children exhibited a thorough contempt for the buddy system from the moment we bought this place. It's as though you wanted to drown, and leave me to explain it to the authorities.

> *A pause. She eats.*

As though your existence revolved around getting me into trouble. Have I ever told you about how we came to own this cottage?

MICHELLE
(still within) I forget. Tell me the one about the car crash instead.

FRANCES
The car crash?

MICHELLE
The New Year's Eve car crash.

FRANCES
Oh. Oh, yes! Good Lord, how did you know about that?

MICHELLE
I forget how I found out about that incident. You were in a car crash?

FRANCES
New Year's Eve, your father a young man, our latest new car, a company car. There was a new one every two years.

MICHELLE
Yes.

FRANCES
It rained while we were at the party.

MICHELLE
It was hardly a party.

FRANCES
Well, it was hardly a party. It would be cruel to call it a party. It was a function. It was dry and efficient and bloodless, and we agreed that "function" was the perfect way to describe it. Your father, in a thin tie, putting his hands on the women's asses; and me, wearing something ghastly and forcing my tongue down the throat of a martini glass to get at the olive. You girls, toddlers I suppose, or less, at home in bed.

And it rained. And then it froze. And we departed after midnight, and your father, attempting to hold me up as we slid downhill, slid further and further away from the car we were trying to get into and start up so as to be safe; your father fell down and cracked his pelvis. He didn't know it then. Cracked his pelvis in two places.

TOM enters. He stands, embarrassed, as she speaks.

And even then, he wouldn't let me drive his precious car. And so it was his inability to sit down properly in the driver's seat or even to use the pedals properly, owing to the severely broken pelvis, that made us sitting ducks, as it were, for the truck that slid through the intersection, coming straight for us. Well. Turning, lazily, like a curling rock, but still, straight for us.

TOM
Frances?

FRANCES
Oh. Tom.

TOM
Were you talking to someone?

FRANCES
You were here.

TOM
Yes, and–

FRANCES
And now you're back.

TOM
    Yes.

FRANCES
    Thank God. I thought I might have just imagined that you were here before. I was asleep, and then you were here.

TOM
    I had the part on the truck.

FRANCES
    You did.

        A beat.

    So you brought it.

TOM
    That's right.

FRANCES
    I see. Well. Hello. Tom.

        A pause.

TOM
    Listen, I–

        MICHELLE walks out, drinking a beer and eating a carrot.

FRANCES
    Oh, dear.

MICHELLE
    Hey, Mr. Ilesic. Didn't you leave?

FRANCES
    He did. And then he came back. He had the part, you see, on the truck.

MICHELLE
    Right on.

FRANCES
    And now he'll leave, and return in the morning to install it.

        FRANCES smiles at TOM.

TOM
    I guess so.

FRANCES
    The mildly incompetent Tom Junior will be waiting.

TOM

Right. See you tomorrow morning.

FRANCES

Yes you will.

TOM leaves.

Excellent timing, as usual, dear. And do you know what I lost as a consequence of that car accident?

MICHELLE

No. Yes. Instincts. The way a person hit on the head loses their sense of smell.

FRANCES

A whole raft of instincts. Instincts for useful life skills. I lost the ability to dress myself and, critically, others, in clothes that weren't filthy. I lost the ability to provide, I lost the ability to be careful. I lost the idea of moderation. I lost the idea that in spite of everything, you have to try. That you have to want to try.

I had no instincts left that might make me a person among people, and yet I forced myself to remain among people. I forced myself to assume a shape, as if assuming might make it real.

A pause.

MICHELLE

And did it?

FRANCES

Hmm? Oh, no dear. Not as such. I mean, ask your fucking father.

A pause.

You seem to have a problem, dear.

MICHELLE

Have I?

FRANCES

Well, haven't you?

MICHELLE

No.

FRANCES

Oh. Well. There you go. No instincts. I rest my handbag.

MICHELLE

I *am* fucking pregnant.

FRANCES
Oh, well.

MICHELLE
Don't tell anybody.

FRANCES
I can't imagine why I would, dear. Or who. But this is awful.

MICHELLE
Well.

FRANCES
You're woefully unqualified. If I may.

MICHELLE laughs.

The sort of thing I'd expect out of your sister. She's the amateur. Is this why you arranged to have us all up here? To tell us?

MICHELLE
You arranged for us all to be up here. You begged us for months.

FRANCES
I did not. I could not care in the least if you and your sister ever set foot on this property again.

MICHELLE
You said if we didn't come out here with you, you'd initiate legal proceedings.

FRANCES
No.

MICHELLE
You did.

FRANCES
No.

A pause.

Did I ever tell you about the time I was sued by Proctor and Gamble?

MICHELLE
Do you have to?

They look each other in the eye.

FRANCES
You know I do. I will unpack my heart. I will divest myself of all this filth, and you can listen or not listen.

MICHELLE
Okay.

FRANCES
Your sister does not understand.

MICHELLE
Okay.

> *MICHELLE looks away and FRANCES resumes her normal tone.*

FRANCES
One day, there was a knock at the door, and a man handed me papers outlining Proctor and Gamble's lawsuit against me. This came completely out of the blue. To be sued by a large corporation: we all know it could happen—most of us believe it's only a matter of time—but I was absolutely shocked.

MICHELLE
Yes.

> *MICHELLE rises and goes inside.*

FRANCES
I had to engage a lawyer, without your father's knowledge. Your father has a disgust for the legal profession that is now only rivalled by mine for him. Do you know, he drew up his will by hand? Literally? He found out that a handwritten will is perfectly legal, and this man who I used to have to hogtie and beat senseless before he'd write a birthday card sat down and wrote out his entire will only so as to thwart our family lawyer.

Proctor and Gamble had letters, they alleged. Letters from me. Threatening letters. From me! It was absurd!

> *MICHELLE re-enters with a fresh beer and a box of salt.*

They produced one of these letters, gave it to my lawyer. Several closely-typed pages, promising violence and accusing Proctor and Gamble of a vast conspiracy. Rambling, lunatic verbiage. And then, there it was: my signature at the bottom.

> *RUNE enters, wrapped in a towel, her night clothes in her hand. She kicks off the running shoes. She sits, and MICHELLE gives her the box of salt. During the following, RUNE pours salt on a good-sized leech that's attached to her calf, waits, then removes the leech.*

I was aware, of course, of the horrifying things Proctor and Gamble was doing. Good God, we all were. I mean, turn on the television. It was common knowledge: the animals they used, the gross financial abuses. The stunted babies. But to say that I was somehow motivated to sit down and write–. *(of the leech)* Isn't that awful, dear.

RUNE pours salt on the leech.

RUNE
No, not really.

They watch the leech for a few beats.

FRANCES
Where was I?

MICHELLE
You were–

RUNE
We don't know. Weren't you listening either?

FRANCES
I–. No, I guess not. *(rising, to RUNE)* Your sister has some news. I forget what.

FRANCES goes inside.

MICHELLE
(after a beat) You have news? Can I guess?

RUNE
I don't.

MICHELLE
I bet I can guess.

RUNE
She said *you* have news.

MICHELLE
Is it about the job?

RUNE
No, I haven't decided about that. And she was talking about you.

MICHELLE
(rising unsteadily) You want a beer?

RUNE
No.

MICHELLE
Sure you do. You have to canoe later.

MICHELLE goes inside. RUNE pours more salt on the dying leech, now curling up on the step beside her. She empties the contents of the box on the leech. MATTHEW appears. He carries a travel coffee mug.

MATTHEW
Hi.

RUNE
Right.

A pause. Nobody moves.

MATTHEW
I hit the hole you have in the driveway.

RUNE
Road.

MATTHEW
I sort of left the car in there.

RUNE
Uh huh.

MATTHEW
I'm not sure it'll come out. I'm pretty sure I broke the floor. Pretty sure I cut my forehead on the steering wheel.

RUNE
Well, nice to see you.

MATTHEW
Nice to see you.

A pause. RUNE gets up, walks around the side of the cottage, takes off the towel and puts on some clothes hanging on the line.

So, anyway, this is it, huh? Man, I'm tired. I drove like all night it felt like.

A pause.

RUNE
Take a swim.

MATTHEW
Yeah.

A pause.

You know what?

RUNE
What.

MATTHEW
I think you should get married.

A pause.

RUNE
What?

MATTHEW
(simultaneous with above line) Shit. I think *we* should get married. I think we should get married. We.

RUNE
Oh.

MATTHEW
Fuck. Ha ha. Nice. How long's the drive up here? Like four hours?

RUNE
Two and a bit.

MATTHEW
It's more like four if you get lost. Four hours practising that. Then I tell *you* to get married.

RUNE, dressed, comes around the side of the cottage.

RUNE
Why.

MATTHEW
Yes. Well, it seems the right thing to do.

RUNE
How so.

MATTHEW
Well, I mean, have you ever felt like this before?

RUNE
Felt like what?

MATTHEW
Like this. You haven't. You haven't felt like this before.

RUNE
How do you know. Oh. I told you.

MATTHEW
You told me.

RUNE
Yes I did.

MATTHEW
Yes.

RUNE
But.

MATTHEW
Yes?

RUNE
But that doesn't mean anything.

MATTHEW
No?

RUNE
It's a thing to say. In that situation.

MATTHEW
It wasn't true?

RUNE
No, it was true. I didn't, I hadn't felt like that. That's true. But so what?

MATTHEW
But, so—

RUNE
Where were you yesterday?

MATTHEW
Yesterday?

RUNE
Fucking yes.

MATTHEW
In bed. Why?

RUNE
You were in bed yesterday?

MATTHEW
Yes. In it, or sitting you know on the edge, looking into my shoes. I also spent some time looking *at* the bed. From a distance. Why?

RUNE
You were supposed to be here yesterday.

MATTHEW
Yesterday?

RUNE
Yes. It's what we said.

MATTHEW
No.

RUNE
Yes.

MATTHEW
Well, not, no.

RUNE
Yes, you stupid–. It was so embarrassing.

MATTHEW
What day is it?

RUNE
I waited all day. It was humiliating.

MATTHEW
You're lucky I didn't come up yesterday. I was a complete mess yesterday. I thought we were going to break up.

A pause. She goes to him, kisses him. She then retreats to the other side of the stage again.

It's nice out here.

RUNE
No it's not.

MATTHEW
No?

RUNE
But it's nice of you to say.

A pause.

I'm sorry. We should get married?

She laughs. They laugh together.

MATTHEW
I was thinking that, yes. It makes all kinds of sense. I mean, neither one of us seems to know what to want. I don't know what I'm doing in law school, you don't seem particularly passionate about whatever

it is you're studying. I assume you still don't have a clue about whether or not to take this job?

RUNE

No.

MATTHEW

No. You're completely ignorant about it. We share that. And into all this ignorance about what to want, about our futures, comes *this*. Prompting you to say things like "I've never felt this way before," which, okay, it's a thing to say, but also, apparently true, and so, it has a great momentum behind it, that; and incidentally I was feeling that as you said it. By the way. I was feeling that, too. You said it, and I thought: "Me too." Or, rather, "Me neither."

RUNE

You said "That's sweet."

MATTHEW

I know.

RUNE

"That's *sweet*."

MATTHEW

I know.

RUNE

Me: "I've never felt this way before." You: "Oh, that's sweet."

MATTHEW

I know. But I was thinking: "Me neither."

RUNE

You incredible jerk.

MATTHEW

No, I know.

> *A pause.*

RUNE

So what if I don't know what I want to do with myself?

MATTHEW

Well, that's *my* point.

RUNE

Like, that's a reason? I tell people that when they ask why I got married?

MATTHEW

Of course not. You'll sound like an idiot.

RUNE

So–

MATTHEW

But you–

RUNE

Just because I don't know what I'm–

MATTHEW

Can I–?

RUNE

What?

MATTHEW

Can I? Because, look. Okay. I have, my parents, they stopped being a couple around 1979. '78 or '79. But before that, they were just... they had this thing about them, an awareness of each other, an understanding, a, a, a thing. And they were better as a team than they were as people. I didn't know that, I couldn't have told you that then, all I knew was they got each other's jokes. They had shorthand. They, worked. They *worked*. They made, as people, a more competent group than they did individuals. On their own, my father, driving all over the city, no sense of direction; my mother, yelling at the dry cleaner for something she'd later admit was probably her fault. Like separately, they weren't menaces or anything, that came later, but they were just better together.

And I have this funny feeling that I will be, too. And you seem, and there seems to be this, momentum, between us, and as far as I can tell, that qualifies us for what they had.

RUNE

Your parents can't stand each other now.

MATTHEW

Well, yes. Try not to focus on that part.

> *A pause.*

RUNE

What will we do?

MATTHEW

Well, you know.

> *A pause.*

RUNE

If I say yes, do you know why?

MATTHEW

Do I know why you'd say yes? Cause it's a helluvan idea, and–

RUNE

No, shut up. Because the morning after we, uh, met, we were sitting outside on a bench and I had to go to I don't know, Western Religions or friggin' Classical Survey or something, and I was talking about my sister, complaining about her, and I could tell you stopped listening. And I thought, fuckin guy, gets what he wants, one night in bed, and he stops listening. And then you said: "You're very well lit."

A pause.

MATTHEW

Well, you are.

RUNE

And I went: "Hey. Wait a minute."

A pause.

You seem so certain.

MATTHEW

I know.

RUNE

It's kinda fuckin' disgusting.

MATTHEW

Don't worry. It won't last.

A pause.

RUNE

I feel like it, okay? And I, and you seem to be making very excellent points. You've clearly had a lot of time to...

And I feel like it. I feel it, too. I do. It's not just something to say. And so, I think, say yes, and I do in my head, and then I go: what's the problem?

MATTHEW

What are you, like scared?

RUNE

Well, sure. Of course. Jesus Christ, Matthew.

MATTHEW
But that's good, probably.

RUNE
But that's not it. That's not the problem. The problem, the problem is…

MATTHEW
You don't have to decide now.

RUNE
No, it's… I don't know who I'd be. I don't know who I'd be.

MATTHEW
You'd be…

RUNE
I mean, I'm nothing now.

MATTHEW
No. No you're not nothing.

RUNE
Well, yes.

MATTHEW
What a thing to say.

RUNE
I don't mind. I mean, I assume I won't always be nothing. But that's why the idea of this seems–.

MATTHEW
Seems.

RUNE
I'm just, I'm not qualified to be making any decisions right now.

MATTHEW
You don't have to decide now.

RUNE
I just did.

MATTHEW
No, you didn't.

RUNE
Yes I did. I love you so much.

MATTHEW
You, what?

RUNE
I do. I love you so much.

MATTHEW
...But.

RUNE
Yes.

A pause.

MATTHEW
I don't understand. You love me so much.

RUNE
I don't, I just, I can't–

MATTHEW
No, I don't want to *understand*. Don't, like, stand there and explain it.

A pause.

Well. So. I'm gonna go sit on the... *(motions toward the dock)*

RUNE
The dock?

MATTHEW
The, yes.

RUNE
Okay. Did you bring a suit?

MATTHEW
I don't know. Did I bring a suit. Um. Against who?

RUNE
No, I mean–

MATTHEW
Oh. Right. Did I–. No. Not really. So. But.

RUNE
Okay. You have to go that way *(indicates off right)* for the path. To get down there. *(indicates the water ahead of them)* Sorry.

He wanders off. A pause. He charges back on again.

MATTHEW
My feeling is, if you *are* nothing, you don't wait to become something, and then do things as that person. You do things, and then you go: "I'm not nothing, I'm the person that did those

things." Otherwise, you stand around for like a fuck of a long time doing nothing.

RUNE
I don't know.

A pause.

MATTHEW
Are you sure?

RUNE
Of course I'm not sure. What kind of a question is that?

MATTHEW
Yes. Sorry.

RUNE
I mean, fuck.

MATTHEW
Yes.

RUNE
I mean, – Matthew?

MATTHEW
Yes?

RUNE
Maybe we...

MATTHEW
Yes?

A longish pause. Finally, FRANCES enters, sees his mug.

FRANCES
Is that coffee?!?

RUNE
(to MATTHEW) No.

MATTHEW
No. Okay. *(to FRANCES)* Hi. No. I'm all out.

FRANCES
Weren't you supposed to be here yesterday?

MATTHEW
I'm gonna go down and sit on the... thing.

He wants to leave, is confused about which way to go.

RUNE

(indicating the path) That way. Sorry.

MATTHEW leaves.

FRANCES

What was his name again?

A pause.

Did your sister tell you her news?

A pause.

I think your sister could use someone to talk to.

RUNE

So talk to her.

FRANCES

Darling. I don't talk to people. Do you really think I was too abrupt with Tom Ilesic?

RUNE

I don't know. I don't know anything.

FRANCES

I know, but I was asking for some speculation. I was actually asking you to pull your head out of your 20-year-old ass and give me a fucking opinion. I don't want you to tell me facts, I don't want you to carve out a plan of action regarding this man, I don't want anything concrete from you, I just want to talk about it. He came back, did you know that? He did. Why would he do that? I want to blather away about it, as is our way, and in the end I suppose I want to figure out, using the most loopy, roundabout methods available, why it is that even though I have no interest in this man, none at all, he suddenly became interesting to me when he showed some interest in me. I guess I want to run all over that a few times, and see how flat I can get it, as it were. I also want, I suppose, to know how a man can seem interested in such an awful, exhausting old woman.

RUNE gets up, hugs her mother.

RUNE

Maybe he's going deaf.

FRANCES

You know, I don't know anything. I don't know anything. How did I get this way? How do you get to be this age and not know anything? Did I know things? Was I a person? How did I get along?

Did I ever know how to see other people? Was it your father? Did
I do something to your father? Did he do something to me?

RUNE

(*adding to her list of questions*) Do you want to have a nap?

FRANCES

Is there still no coffee?

RUNE

Do you smell any coffee?

FRANCES

There still not being coffee is a sign of contempt, you know. For your
mother.

RUNE

That's exactly right, sweetie.

> *FRANCES rises.*

FRANCES

I'm going to lie down. Oh. Your sister's pregnant. Help her.

> *FRANCES goes inside. As she does:*

Michelle! Get out here! Your sister has something to tell you.

> *RUNE takes several steps away from the cottage, looking toward
> the dock. MICHELLE plunges out the door, misjudging the step
> down to the porch. She's scrutinising several pills in her hand.*

MICHELLE

The fuck is that one? Can you identify it?

> *RUNE goes to her.*

RUNE

Is that ecstasy?

MICHELLE

Fuck that.

> *MICHELLE tosses the pill away. While it's still in the air:*

No!

> *MICHELLE follows the pill, which has landed in a bush. She
> begins to look for it.*

RUNE

Mother says you told her you're pregnant.

MICHELLE
Do you know why she told you that?

RUNE
No.

MICHELLE
Because she has a big, cavernous, needy fucking mouth.

RUNE
Yes.

MICHELLE
And she doesn't understand the notion of confidence. Of when she's being taken into a confidence. No idea how to be of any use at all, how to try to be of use to a person, and really no idea at all *(She has turned and yells briefly at the cottage.)* HOW TO MAKE AN EFFORT.

> *A pause. MICHELLE looks for the pill.*

RUNE
Is it true?

> *A pause. MICHELLE finds the pill, regards it.*

MICHELLE
Yes.

> *MICHELLE swallows the ecstasy.*

RUNE
What are you going to do?

MICHELLE
Well. I'm going to take everything I can get my hands on over the next few months, by way of introduction. And then, if it still wants to come out, I'll have a thing. A baby.

> *A pause.*

MICHELLE
Then I'll be the mother.

Who the fuck is that?

RUNE
It's Matt. He showed up.

MICHELLE
It's Matt? *The* Matt?

RUNE
> He proposed.

MICHELLE
> To you?

RUNE
> Yes.

MICHELLE
> Well... what did you say?

RUNE
> I don't know.

> *A pause. From the dock, MATTHEW cries "Aw, Jesus!"*

MICHELLE
> He proposed marriage?

RUNE
> Yes.

MICHELLE
> Nobody proposes marriage. Huh. Nice move. Uh oh. Here he comes. Just act natural.

> *MICHELLE rises, moves about aimlessly, settles. MATTHEW enters, pants rolled up, shoes off, with a leech attached to a leg. To RUNE:*

MATTHEW
> I didn't even go in. I didn't even touch the bottom. I was just sitting there, you know, dangling over the side, and it found me. Latched onto me. I... can you get it off? I'm, I can't look at it. I'm gonna puke.

> *He sits.*

RUNE
> Okay. Just a sec. I'll get some salt.

> *RUNE goes inside. MICHELLE moves into MATTHEW's view.*

MATTHEW
> Oh. Hi.

MICHELLE
> I'm pregnant.

> *A pause.*

MATTHEW
Oh no.

A pause.

MICHELLE
Really, any response you might have had would seem inadequate, but that one was *really*, don't you think?

MATTHEW
I'm sorry. I… what are you going to do?

MICHELLE
Nothing.

MATTHEW
Nothing?

MICHELLE
No. Nothing.

A pause.

MATTHEW
What do you mean, when you say "nothing," because I don't know if I–

MICHELLE
No. It's done. I wanted to tell you, and see what you would have to say, but really, you can consider the whole thing over. Terminated.

MATTHEW
Terminated?

MICHELLE
Yes. Terminated. As far as you, Matthew Somethingsomething, is concerned. I terminated it.

MATTHEW
Oh. Michelle. Oh.

MICHELLE
Sorry to have brought it up. Thank you for being so clear. You proposed to her?

MATTHEW
Michelle.

MICHELLE
You proposed to my sister. It's sweet. You're the guy who's sweet.

MATTHEW
Michelle, listen–

MICHELLE
You have to shut up now.

RUNE enters with a box of matches.

RUNE
We're out of salt. But we can burn it off. Hold still.

RUNE strikes a match, and MATTHEW offers his leg. He looks away. Unfortunately, MICHELLE is in his field of vision when he does so, and they lock eyes. A pause. MATTHEW flinches, moves his leg and is burned.

MATTHEW
Ah!! Crap!!

RUNE
Sorry, sorry!

FRANCES
(from inside) What's happening?

RUNE
Sorry!

FRANCES
(from inside) What's going on? I was still asleep!

RUNE
Hold still.

MATTHEW
Sorry. Sorry.

MICHELLE
You'd better hold still. You'd better not, you know, move, mister. She's got you now.

RUNE strikes another match, slowly approaches MATTHEW's leg. FRANCES appears at the screen door.

FRANCES
WHAT'S GOING ON?!?

RUNE
Nothing. Be quiet. Jesus.

FRANCES
I WILL NOT BE QUIET. DON'T YOU TELL ME TO BE QUIET.
I WAS ASLEEP.

MICHELLE
Mother–

FRANCES
I don't know if you know just how startling it is to be asleep and
then violently startled awake. You people shout constantly, you make
noise above me just when you think I don't know who it will be. You
do it on purpose. You do it on purpose! You–

MICHELLE
–do it on purpose. All right. It's clear, okay? You're being quite clear.
You just woke up, okay? You're awake now. It's okay. You can go back
to bed now. Go back to bed.

FRANCES
I can't sleep. What's going on here?

FRANCES comes outside.

RUNE
(to MATTHEW) Hold still.

FRANCES
Who is this?

MATTHEW
Hello, Mrs. Arlidge.

FRANCES
I thought I said no visitors? I thought I said no people?

MATTHEW
Sorry, I just, um, ow!

The match burns RUNE, and she drops it.

RUNE
Fuck.

FRANCES
All I wanted was to not have to worry about people. I wanted time
for the three of us. I wanted the three of us to be together. I wanted–

MICHELLE
Mother.

FRANCES

I wanted to have you here. I wanted to have you, just us. I told you that.

MICHELLE

It's okay.

FRANCES

No, it's not okay. I told her what I wanted, I told you both. But she never sees it. She's so busy with her, her life that she makes no allowances for me or for us. You know it's true.

RUNE

(removing the leech) Got it.

MICHELLE

Mother.

FRANCES

She's an awful person. She used to be so loving, she used to be a sweet little kid, and now, she's become this thing nobody recognises. *(wheels on RUNE)* It's true. You used to be so helpful and sweet and all the time we worried about her, we knew you'd never do anything as awful as her. You were the one. What happened? What happened to you? Answer me! I'm going to die, do you know that? Answer me!

RUNE

(to MATTHEW) You should go.

MATTHEW

Okay, yes.

FRANCES

Don't you see what you were? Don't you see what we wanted? How can you do that? How can you do that? Why can't you help anyone? It's, you're infuriating me! Why do you do that?

RUNE

I'm coming too.

MATTHEW

Okay.

FRANCES

You what? Oh, no you're not, young lady. You've got a fucking canoe to paddle.

RUNE

I'm ready now.

MATTHEW
>Oh? Okay.

FRANCES
>You have always been the most selfish, awful child. You're needed. Don't you see you're needed here? I'm going to die. Your sister needs you. Your sister.

MICHELLE
>MOTHER.

MATTHEW
>What about your stuff?

RUNE
>I'm ready now.

FRANCES
>Did you hear me? I'm going to–

RUNE
>NO YOU'RE NOT.

>*RUNE rises and walks off. MATTHEW rises.*

FRANCES
>Where does she think she's going?

MICHELLE
>Get the fuck out of here.

MATTHEW
>Michelle, let me–

MICHELLE
>No! You have to *leave me alone.*

>*MATTHEW exits.*

FRANCES
>That's right. You're not the only one with needs. I'm not the only one with needs. What about her? Hey? RUNE? HELP YOUR SISTER. RUNE: WHY DON'T YOU HELP YOUR SISTER??

>*A pause.*

>What time is it? What's that smell? What got burned?

>*Blackout.*

Act Two

The same, ten years later. The cottage has slid a foot to the left. Paint has peeled, foliage has encroached. Mid-afternoon, the height of summer. FRANCES sits in her seat on the porch, in loose clothing. A series of strokes have left her nearly immobile and without speech. She weeps freely throughout the act, and will grunt at points but never speak. The lights snap up and we see HARVAR, 38, wearing only a Speedo. He has the makings of a pot belly, red hair and is suntan oily. He holds two hot dogs, and is offering one to LILLIAN, 10.

HARVAR
Want one?

LILLIAN
What are they?

HARVAR
What do you mean, what are they. It's a hot dog. Do you want it or not?

LILLIAN
What will you do if I say no?

HARVAR
What do you mean what will I do. I'll eat it.

LILLIAN
No, the other one.

HARVAR
I'll eat it, too. Do you want it?

LILLIAN
You'll eat both?

HARVAR
Do you want one or not?

LILLIAN
No way. I want to see you eat both.

HARVAR
Okay. Suit yourself. Where was I?

LILLIAN
The guy with the beard?

HARVAR
Oh yeah. So, I'm sitting there, and he's talking away, and the bartender is bringing us drinks, without our asking for them, they just come from like out of nowhere, and I'm like: "Great," and then a couple of hours later, the guy's girlfriend comes in. Dressed just like him. You know, vest, tattoos, leather chaps and the whole bit. And she is hot. She's like stripper hot. And suddenly I go: "Holy shit. They aren't motorcycle enthusiasts. They're like bikers!" I been drinking for four hours with a biker! I threw a rock at a biker, and I picked a fight with a biker, and now I'm sitting drinking with a biker and his girlfriend.

LILLIAN
No way.

HARVAR
I shit you not.

LILLIAN
What's a biker?

HARVAR
What? How old are you.

LILLIAN
Nearly ten. I have a bike.

HARVAR
No no no. Bikers ride motorcycles and they control all the criminal activity in Quebec and also here. They sell drugs and push people around and that sort of thing. They like kill people.

LILLIAN
They kill people?

HARVAR
They totally kill people. They mostly try to kill other bikers, but sometimes the general public gets in the way and then they get killed, too.

LILLIAN
Okay.

HARVAR

So, I'm sitting there, right? And suddenly I'm going over the whole afternoon in my head, trying to figure out if there's anything I said that would make a biker mad. Like, I kind of told him some things, you know how you do, when you're sitting in a bar with a stranger and you get talking, not necessarily all the things that come out of your mouth are completely true?

LILLIAN

Right.

HARVAR

So, I'm talking away, and I'm drinking, and I'm thinking about what I've already said, and I'm trying to think if I'm getting myself into more trouble here, I mean, I already picked a fight with the guy, and I threw a rock at him, and so maybe he's just filling time drinking with me, you know, pretending to be nice, while actually he's going to kill me for throwing a rock at him. So my brain is suddenly working like really hard, I'm sweating, and trying to talk away to the guy in a calm, friendly way, and all of a sudden, I feel something against my leg.

LILLIAN

What.

HARVAR

Exactly. That's what I'd like to know. It's rubbing up and down against my leg, under the table. And then a guy comes up to talk to the biker guy, and while he's distracted, the girlfriend winks at me.

LILLIAN

She winks at you?

HARVAR

The biker's girlfriend like totally winks at me. I shit you not.

LILLIAN

Like this?

LILLIAN tries to wink.

HARVAR

Sort of. And I. Freak. Out.

LILLIAN

I bet.

HARVAR

Do you know how dead I'd be if the guy finds out his girlfriend has the hots for me? But, also, I'm a little drunk, too, so I think: "Hey.

Maybe this is something I can actually get away with. Maybe I can get it on with the biker chick and the boyfriend will never know." Like, that's how drunk I am. By the way, this is way before I met your aunt, okay?

LILLIAN
Okay.

HARVAR
We had not even met yet, okay?

LILLIAN
Okay.

HARVAR
Okay. So she's rubbing up against me and she's showing me her tattoos, and then the guy goes to the bathroom. And she leans toward me, real close, and I lean in, too, and I notice she's got a lot of makeup on, right? And then I look at her throat, and I notice she's got like an adam's apple, except it's covered with lots of makeup, right? But I'm so drunk I don't really get what I'm seeing, right? So–

LILLIAN
Eat the other one.

HARVAR
What? Oh, no, I don't want it.

LILLIAN
You said you would.

HARVAR
No, five's my limit. Here.

LILLIAN
I can't eat it.

HARVAR
Go ahead. You must be starved. All you do is swim all day.

LILLIAN
Okay.

> *LILLIAN takes the hot dog.*

HARVAR
So, where was I?

LILLIAN
I don't know.

HARVAR

Oh, yeah, so the girlfriend is rubbing all over me, looking at me, the whole bit, and suddenly–

MICHELLE

(from inside the cottage) Lillian!

> *MICHELLE comes out onto the porch. She has white, creased pants on, and shoes inappropriate for a cottage. As she speaks, she rests a hand on FRANCES' shoulder.*

What is that?

LILLIAN

He gave it to me.

MICHELLE

You know you can't eat that. Good God, Harvar, she can't eat that.

HARVAR

No, it's okay. I'm full.

MICHELLE

Give me that.

> *LILLIAN gives MICHELLE the hot dog, which MICHELLE holds behind her back for the rest of her time on the porch.*

Your lunch will be ready at one o'clock, young lady.

LILLIAN

Okay.

MICHELLE

Are you hungry now? Do you want a carrot?

LILLIAN

No.

MICHELLE

(to HARVAR) Is she bothering you?

HARVAR

No. Not really. Where's Rune?

MICHELLE

Don't bother the adults, darling. Don't you feel like swimming?

LILLIAN

No.

MICHELLE
Well, don't bother the adults. *(She leans over FRANCES.)* Mother? Do you want anything?

FRANCES grimaces.

Where's your hat?

FRANCES grunts with displeasure, and MICHELLE finds the straw hat and puts it on her head.

There you go. I'll bring you something to eat in a minute.

HARVAR
Hey, Michelle?

MICHELLE
Yes?

HARVAR
Where's Rune?

MICHELLE
We're doing the family accounts.

HARVAR
So, what, she's inside?

MICHELLE
Yes.

HARVAR
Okay.

MICHELLE
Did you want her?

HARVAR
No, I just, I thought I lost her there for a second. Okay.

MICHELLE
(to LILLIAN) Come inside for a carrot.

LILLIAN
Okay.

HARVAR
Michelle, what are you going to do with that hot dog?

MICHELLE
Do you want it?

HARVAR
Do you want it?

> *A beat. She hands him the hot dog and goes inside. HARVAR takes a bite of the second hot dog, and then puts it down.*

Hand me those sunglasses, okay?

> *LILLIAN gets the sunglasses. As she does so, she walks past FRANCES. She removes FRANCES' hat and throws it on the ground. She delivers the sunglasses.*

LILLIAN
These are cool.

HARVAR
Those are John Cusack's business manager's sunglasses. He left them in the back of my car.

LILLIAN
Cool.

> *A pause. HARVAR has reclined.*

So, what about the guy with the beard?

HARVAR
(without sitting up) Hmm? Oh, it was a real mess. It went on and on, for like 36 hours. Ended in a motel room in Hull. I'll tell you sometime.

MICHELLE
(from the cottage) Lillian!

LILLIAN
Coming!

> *LILLIAN rises immediately and exits toward the water instead. A pause. FRANCES watches HARVAR closely. RUNE comes out of the cottage. She is brittle, and slightly nervous. She manages to ignore FRANCES utterly. She goes to HARVAR, stands over him.*

HARVAR
Hey!

RUNE
Hi. How are you?

HARVAR
I'm fantastic. How are you?

> *HARVAR gets up and kisses RUNE.*

RUNE

Tremendous. Do you want a beer?

HARVAR

Of course I want a beer. Did you bring me a beer?

RUNE

No, but I can.

HARVAR

Or, I can get it.

RUNE

No, I'll get it. I should have brought one with me.

HARVAR

Why? I've got two legs.

RUNE

I know, but I brought it up.

HARVAR

No, it's, really, it's okay. I'll get it. Sit down. How's it going in there?

RUNE

It's wonderful fun. Bank accounts with six dollars each in them scattered around the city. That sort of thing.

HARVAR

It's like that show.

RUNE

What show.

HARVAR

The one where the people go all over town to get things like, you know, six dollars out of a bank account. It's a race.

RUNE

You're kidding.

HARVAR

You've seen it. It's hosted by that guy, what's his name, I had him in my car once...

RUNE

It's hosted by John Travolta?

HARVAR

No, not John Travolta. Never mind. Do you want a hot dog, sweetie?

RUNE
Hmm. No thanks.

HARVAR
You got to get a barbecue up here.

RUNE
It's true.

HARVAR
And a, like a hammock for between those two trees.

RUNE
Yes.

HARVAR
And a jet ski.

RUNE
Oh yeah. And a functioning toilet.

HARVAR
Oh, yeah. I was gonna fix that.

RUNE
No, it's okay. Someone's going to come later and do it.

HARVAR
But I said I would.

RUNE
I know. Nobody took you seriously. It's okay. Don't tell Lillian the biker story, okay?

HARVAR
I wasn't.

RUNE
Yeah, you were.

HARVAR
Well, she makes me nervous. She's a weird little kid.

RUNE
Yes.

HARVAR
I feel like I have to keep talking or she'll do something.

A pause.

RUNE
I spoke to your mother yesterday. About the wedding.

HARVAR

Jesus Christ. I'm sorry.

RUNE

She either wants to invite seven more people, or seventeen. I couldn't figure it out due to the *tick Norwegian ec-cent.*

HARVAR

I don't believe this. I'm sorry. I'll get on the phone and bitchslap her.

RUNE

No, it's okay.

HARVAR

No, she's got to shut up about the wedding. Honest to God. Could she be any more Jewish? I'll call her, tell her to shut her piehole. Gawd.

RUNE

I actually like talking to your mother.

HARVAR

Yes. You're very polite to her. You're like the first one of my girlfriends she can stand for more than five minutes. I think she likes you more than she likes me. Lucky fucking you.

RUNE

Your mother is funny. She's not that bad.

HARVAR

Yeah, well, try telling her you're dropping out of high school to sell drugs full time, and then see how you like her. It doesn't matter that I only did that for a few years. And never got caught, I might add. As far as Elva's concerned, I'm a career Colombian drug lord for life. Good thing I found me a girl with a respectable job.

RUNE

It's actually not all that respectable.

HARVAR

Sure it is. Telling people what you think, week after week. This guy's great because he like built a shelter for the homeless, this guy's an asshole cause he's fucking up the environment; believe this, don't believe that. Newspapers are great. Even the little hippie ones, like yours.

RUNE

Not that you read them.

HARVAR

Fuck no. But still, it's like a total public service, telling people what to think.

RUNE

Not everyone considers it a public service. You know the mail I get.

HARVAR

You still getting the ones where people tell you and your commie friends to burn in the piss rivers of damnation? I love those.

RUNE

I had one from a guy who was so incensed about my views on same-sex marriage that he wanted to violate me anally.

HARVAR

Already? I just put that in the mail like Tuesday.

RUNE

I didn't know you wanted to violate me anally.

HARVAR

Well, I don't know. I probably do. What exactly does violate mean again?

RUNE

What did you do with that dictionary I gave you?

HARVAR

I sold it. That was a dictionary?

RUNE

Oh my God.

HARVAR

Oh my God. Rune Arlidge.

A pause.

RUNE

Listen, Harvar…

HARVAR

Oh, fuck. Yes?

RUNE

Can we talk about your bachelor party?

HARVAR

What. We're not going to do anything.

MICHELLE comes outside with a carrot.

MICHELLE

Lillian! Lillian! Do you think I peeled this for my health? *(to RUNE and HARVAR)* Honest to God.

LILLIAN

(from off) Okay.

HARVAR

What's that you're playing with there Michelle? Made a new friend?

MICHELLE

Look, stop telling my daughter biker stories, okay?

HARVAR

She started it.

MICHELLE

Did she.

HARVAR

Yeah. She said "Mommy loves the part where you cold-cock the biker chick with the bag of frozen peas."

MICHELLE

I do not.

HARVAR

You love it. You know you do. *(rises)* I'm getting a beer. Anyone else?

MICHELLE

No thank you.

RUNE

No.

HARVAR

(yelling) Lilly! You want a beer?

LILLIAN

(from off) What?

HARVAR

Do! You! Want!–

MICHELLE

Never mind!

HARVAR *goes indoors.*

RUNE

You could be nicer to him.

MICHELLE
No, I could not.

MICHELLE puts FRANCES' hat back on.

Are you okay? Do you want to go inside?

FRANCES grunts in the negative.

Do you want to go to sleep?

FRANCES grunts.

Don't tell me to fuck myself. I'm the only one in this family who pays any attention to you.

FRANCES grunts.

Oh, yes it is. It's absolutely true. You know it's true. Do you want to have a nap or not?

FRANCES grunts again, struggles to rise. MICHELLE helps her. When MICHELLE is close enough, FRANCES grabs her hair and pulls. MICHELLE screams. FRANCES won't let go. RUNE ignores the event. HARVAR runs outside.

HARVAR
Jesus! Leave the old lady alone!

MICHELLE
She pulled my hair!

HARVAR
I was talking to your mother.

Frances! Come inside. Here we go. I have some delicious crystal meth I want you to try. That's it. Right this way. Just ignore those horrible daughters of yours. What the hell did you do to deserve children like these, anyway? You kill somebody?

FRANCES and HARVAR go inside.

MICHELLE
God. I don't know why I–. I swear to God, that's it. I can't handle her anymore. I never could handle her.

RUNE
No.

MICHELLE
She was never the least bit appreciative, and now she's becoming violent.

RUNE
Yes.

MICHELLE
What the hell are we going to do about her?

RUNE will not respond. There is a pause.

Can I ask you something? It's gonna sound weird.

RUNE
Is it about her?

MICHELLE
No.

RUNE
Okay.

MICHELLE
It's a feeling I have. You know how Lilly has been a sort of awful child since birth?

RUNE
No.

MICHELLE
Yes you do. She has. She doesn't listen, and she's willful, and it's just on and on with her. You don't know. You never see it. That's what I want to talk to you about. She's that way, all the time, except when anyone else is around. She's awful. She is. Unless somebody other than me is there to see it. We can scream and scream at each other for hours, and as soon as the door opens and someone walks in, she's sweet as can be.

RUNE
Yes, you've told me this.

MICHELLE
I know. I know you don't believe me. But listen, and just tell me if this sounds paranoid–

RUNE
Yes, it does.

MICHELLE
Just listen. I think it's not that she remembers how to be a decent human being when other people show up, I think she does it on purpose. I think she might be doing it on purpose. And if that's true, then do you know what that means?

RUNE
What does it mean.

MICHELLE
It means she's worse than a bad kid. It means she's actually, like, evil. She has evil intent against me. I know how that sounds.

RUNE
You don't know how that sounds, or you wouldn't say it.

MICHELLE
I know. I know. And yet, I can't shake the feeling that she's actually doing something here, something long-term and, well, evil. And I'm the only one who sees it.

RUNE
Michelle.

MICHELLE
Okay, okay. Fine. Forget it. Forget I said anything. I'm just the crazy lady with the totally sweet daughter.

RUNE
Do you want her to come and stay with me for a while?

MICHELLE
Look, it's bad enough I don't have anyone to talk to in this family, you don't need to compound things by taking my daughter away.

RUNE
No one's trying to–

MICHELLE
Thanks very much. I mean, fuck. I try and try and I get no help with any of it. I couldn't be more alone. You know? I could not be more alone. Never mind.

> *MICHELLE rises. LILLIAN enters, wet from swimming and wrapped in a towel. She's also wearing old, beat-up running shoes which are soaking wet.*

(hands her the carrot) Here.

LILLIAN
Thanks for the carrot.

RUNE
(rising) Lilly, just stay put, okay? Eat the carrot, and just stay there.

LILLIAN
What's wrong?

RUNE

It's okay. There's a leech on your leg. Wait here.

MICHELLE

Oh my God!

> *MICHELLE grabs LILLIAN's head and holds it to her to keep her from looking down. LILLIAN eats the carrot. RUNE goes inside.*

It's okay. It's okay, Lilly.

LILLIAN

I know.

MICHELLE

Don't look down.

LILLIAN

Can I ask you something?

MICHELLE

What is it, Lilly?

LILLIAN

You aren't going to try for Harvar, are you?

> *A beat. MICHELLE is stunned by this. After a moment, the door busts open, HARVAR and RUNE come out, RUNE with salt.*

HARVAR

Let me see. Oh crap! That is like the most disgusting thing I've ever seen. Lilly, it looks like a big, black tit is sucking all the blood out of your system. That's exactly what it looks like, a huge black blobby tit that's getting fatter and fatter on the blood of a little girl. Has she passed out yet?

LILLIAN

Yes!

HARVAR

I am seriously going to be sick. That's disgusting. Oh my God. How much blood loss can a girl sustain before she dies, I wonder? How much do you weigh?

LILLIAN

I weigh 88 pounds.

HARVAR

Not anymore you don't. This reminds me of a girl I knew, growing up in Oslo, and she–

RUNE

You grew up in Scarborough.

HARVAR

And this girl, Priscilla her name was, she went swimming in a fjord and she had just gotten her period for the first time and the leeches were just—

LILLIAN screams, RUNE and MICHELLE yell "Shut up!"

I know! Gross, eh? Oh, well. It was nice knowing you, sweetie.

HARVAR returns inside.

MICHELLE

Honest to God.

RUNE

I know. Very *matoor.*

HARVAR

(from inside) I heard that! Whatever it means.

RUNE

Here we go.

The leech falls off. MICHELLE wipes away a bit of blood remaining. LILLIAN removes the sneakers.

MICHELLE

Go get changed now. I'll make your lunch.

LILLIAN goes indoors.

Look, forget I said anything, okay? I didn't mean it.

RUNE

Okay. I'm sorry. Nobody thinks you're nuts.

MICHELLE

Yeah, right. Will you come in and deal with mother while I get lunch?

RUNE

Michelle, I have to—

MICHELLE

Please.

MICHELLE goes inside. RUNE hesitates, then sits down. HARVAR comes out, wearing a t-shirt and drinking a beer.

HARVAR
Hey.

RUNE
Hey.

> *HARVAR sits beside RUNE, kisses her.*

HARVAR
Oh, crap. You want a beer?

RUNE
No.

HARVAR
Here. Take this one. I'll get another.

RUNE
No, it's okay, I don't want one.

HARVAR
Sorry. Sometimes I'm a pig.

> *A pause.*

I got burnt.

RUNE
You did?

> *HARVAR lifts his shirt.*

HARVAR
Look at this. You've got to tell me, you know. You've got to make sure I don't spend too long in the sun. It's a wife's job, you know.

RUNE
Is it.

HARVAR
Absolutely.

RUNE
Well, I'm not your wife yet, mister.

HARVAR
And my job is to tell you that you don't look fat in your new pants.

RUNE
I see.

> *A pause.*

HARVAR
Everything okay?

RUNE
Hmm? Yes.

HARVAR
Is it the bachelor party? I swear to God, it's just going to be beer and poker. And dancers. That's all. No hookers. Some hookers might come, okay, because they're my clients, but just as guests. I swear to God. And I won't let Andy or PJ or Bishy or any of those guys get outta hand, okay? No matter how drunk we get, I won't let them talk me into anything stupid, okay? Okay?

RUNE
It's okay.

HARVAR
Not it's not. It bothers you. I thought I'd finally found someone that wouldn't be bothered by this kind of shit, but it looks like not. Ah well, what the fuck. Why should I be the first guy in history?

RUNE
Really, I don't mind. I'd prefer it didn't happen the night before the rehearsal, that's all.

HARVAR
But, there's nothing I can do about that.

RUNE
I know, I know.

HARVAR
Look, either you trust me or you don't.

RUNE
That's the stupidest thing you've said in a while.

HARVAR
What?

RUNE
Nothing.

HARVAR
Did you just call me stupid?

RUNE
No. *No.* I just said that that was a stupid thing to say. Trust comes and goes, it's there or not there, you know, it's untrustworthy. It's an idea. It's not a fact.

HARVAR has risen; he's suddenly upset.

HARVAR

(He drops his voice.) Look, okay? I want to say–. I know who I am
in this, okay? I know that I'm the stupid one in this relationship.
I know that. But you can't use stupid on me like that.

RUNE

What's wrong?

HARVAR

I just, I have the feeling that the way we work is if neither of us
notices that there's this huge difference between us. I mean, if I was
like a fat fucking pig, and you were just normal sized, you could
never, ever call me fat, you know? So...

RUNE

Okay.

HARVAR

Do you know what I mean?

RUNE

Sort of. Okay. I'm sorry.

HARVAR

Okay.

He sits down again.

You can call me fucking fatty as much as you want, by the way.

RUNE

Great.

HARVAR

Unless I get fat.

RUNE

Right.

A pause.

HARVAR

Um. Hey. Do you know who Don McKellar is?

RUNE

Sort of.

HARVAR

Did I ever tell you about the time Don McKellar held me up at
gunpoint?

RUNE

I don't think so.

HARVAR

Film festival, three or four years ago. I'm working eighteen, twenty hours a day for like three weeks. Last night of the festival, I'm so tired I can't even see straight, I mean, I've been eating bennies for days but still, and I'm parked in front of like Roy Thomson Hall, and Don McKellar gets into my car and starts screaming at me, right? "Drive! Drive, motherfucker, drive!" And, like, it's not his car, right? I'm there waiting for what'shisname, the guy from TV, the chunky guy, the bald guy?

RUNE

Uh huh.

HARVAR

You know who I mean?

RUNE

Sure.

HARVAR

So I say: "Look, man, I'm sorry, but I'm not your ride, okay dude?" And Don McKellar starts to cry. Honest to God starts to cry in the back of my car. So I go: "Hey, it's okay there, little buddy, just sit there, take as long as you like, get your shit together." And he sits there, and gets himself together, and he's about to go, and then he starts crying again. So then—

RUNE

Harvar.

HARVAR

Yes?

RUNE

You don't have to entertain me, you know.

HARVAR

No, I know. Okay. Thanks. So then he's like: "Okay, sorry, whatever," and he gets out of the car. But then he jumps into the front seat and pulls out a gun, and I have to drive him to like Burlington. And he's all—

RUNE

Harvar?

HARVAR

Rune Arlidge?

RUNE
Why do you want this?

A pause.

HARVAR
Well, um, shit. I don't know. I guess because you're fantastic. And you love me. And I'm like thirty-eight.

RUNE
Okay.

HARVAR
Okay?

RUNE
Okay.

A pause.

HARVAR
Should I ask you that?

RUNE
No. It's okay.

HARVAR
No, but really. I suddenly feel like I should ask you that. Suddenly, I'm going: "what the fuck is she doing with me?" You know? Like, it's a little fuckin' late, but that never even occurred to me before. You always seemed just to be there, and to be, you know, *there*. If you know what I mean. Since we met.

RUNE
Yes.

HARVAR
So?

RUNE
So?

HARVAR
So what are you doing with me?

RUNE
What am I doing with you?

HARVAR
Yeah.

A pause. RUNE goes to him.

RUNE
Whatever I want.

She kisses him.

HARVAR
Right on.

From in the house:

MICHELLE
You are not done your lunch, young lady!!

HARVAR
So, when's the toilet guy coming? I'm pushing cotton here.

RUNE
He should have been here by now.

HARVAR
Damn.

MICHELLE
Come back here!

LILLIAN
(also inside) No way.

RUNE
There's always the woods.

MICHELLE
You are not excused. Don't be so awful, come back here.

LILLIAN
No way.

HARVAR
No fuckin' *way.*

MICHELLE
You're driving me out of my mind! Sit down!

LILLIAN
If you didn't want me, why did you have me?

MICHELLE
Who knew that it would be you?

LILLIAN bursts outdoors.

HARVAR
How was lunch?

LILLIAN
Lunch was very nice, thank you.

HARVAR
I bet. What'd you have?

LILLIAN
Chickpea and lentil patty.

HARVAR
You're shitting me.

RUNE
Harvar.

HARVAR
No, I'm serious, that's totally child abuse. It's the summer, for God's sake.

RUNE
It's what she and Michelle eat.

LILLIAN
It's what we eat.

HARVAR
No, but I know, but look: it leads to a warped view of your like life, and then you get out in the world, and you look around, and you freak out. It's like, well, it's like–. Okay, look. One day my father comes home and there's this girl at the house, she's I guess about seventeen, I forget her name, and she's supposed to be there every night because my mother has a job, right? She's there to make dinner, okay?

RUNE
You had servants?

HARVAR
No, she was like, she made dinner.

LILLIAN
(to RUNE) She was a cook.

HARVAR
No, she just–. And so, anyway, I'm like I don't know, eleven or something.

MICHELLE
(from inside) Rune!

HARVAR

And I wind up upstairs with her, fooling around, and my dad comes home and fires the girl and says to me: "That's it. No sex for you until you're sixteen." Which is ridiculous, right?

RUNE

Is this story appropriate?

HARVAR

It's totally about what I'm talking about. So when I finally hit sixteen, I just freak out, like, if you know what I mean, and my grades go bad, and everything. In fact, that's when the whole thing started. All the shit that took all these years to straighten out.

MICHELLE

Ow! Jesus! Rune!

> *RUNE gets up.*

HARVAR

One day after you leave home, you're gonna walk into a Taco Bell and you won't come out for like two years. Is all I'm saying.

> *RUNE goes inside. A pause.*

Sorry about that story. It might not have been appropriate.

LILLIAN

No, it was good. I wish we had a cook.

> *A pause.*

Why's it called a honeymoon, do you know?

HARVAR

No idea. Honey. Moon. No idea. Your mom might know.

LILLIAN

No, she doesn't. Where are you guys going again?

HARVAR

I don't know. Like Europe. Your aunt pretty much picked it.

LILLIAN

Don't you care?

HARVAR

Sure. But it's kind of her thing, you know? It's all sort of her thing.

LILLIAN

Getting married?

HARVAR
Generally speaking, it's the girl's thing.

LILLIAN
Or the woman's.

HARVAR
Exactly.

LILLIAN
But you proposed.

HARVAR
Well, no, not really.

LILLIAN
She proposed?

HARVAR
Well, we were talking, and it sort of came up. We both agreed, though.

LILLIAN
That's good.

> *A pause. LILLIAN puts the sneakers on.*

My mother says she can't believe you'd get married.

HARVAR
She said that?

LILLIAN
Yes.

HARVAR
And what did she mean by that, do you think?

LILLIAN
I don't know. She said you still had stuff in you. Do you want to go for a swim?

HARVAR
Not right now. I'm fighting with those hot dogs.

> *LILLIAN goes to the dock. A pause. MICHELLE comes out to the porch. She sits.*

Lentil patties? Are you nuts?

> *MICHELLE begins to cry.*

MICHELLE
Probably. It's good food, though, it's good for–.

HARVAR
What?

MICHELLE
Fuck.

    She turns away.

HARVAR
You okay?

MICHELLE
I'm just–.

HARVAR
Um, what's wrong?

MICHELLE
What's wrong is my fucking mother hates my guts.

HARVAR
No, she doesn't. She's just, she's fucking pissed off at having to sit there like that all day.

MICHELLE
I hate it. I hate it. She needs me and she hates it. I hate that people like you are so fucking understanding of her. Of her terrible situation.

HARVAR
Well, yours kind of blows, too. Anybody can see that.

MICHELLE
Really?

HARVAR
Of course. It's just that nobody gives a shit about you.

MICHELLE
That's right.

HARVAR
You know, where I come from, we put the old people into the leakiest, shittiest boats in the village and push them out into the sea.

MICHELLE
Really.

HARVAR
We get them drunk, give 'em a handjob, and then off they go. Sometimes it's really sick, right, because sometimes the tide pushes them back to the shore, so we have to go down the beach, push them out again, over and over, like maybe ten times.

MICHELLE
Really.

HARVAR
And they're like crying and begging and everything: "Please, don pus me beck to da sea!" It's fuckin' awful.

MICHELLE
Sounds like it.

HARVAR
But really quite beautiful, in its way.

MICHELLE
Who the fuck *are* you?

HARVAR
Yeah, I know.

> *A pause.*

You're gonna be okay.

MICHELLE
I don't know.

HARVAR
Yeah, you are.

> *He goes to her, awkwardly. There's an intimate moment between them, which expires in a pause.*

MICHELLE
You've very good with Lilly.

HARVAR
No I'm not.

MICHELLE
Yes you are.

HARVAR
Your daughter scares the shit out of me, actually.

MICHELLE
You have trouble taking compliments, don't you?

HARVAR

I don't know. I guess so. I've always been a self-defecating kind of guy.

MICHELLE laughs. HARVAR seems confused by her laughter. The sound of a truck pulling up.

Is this the toilet guy?

MICHELLE

Yes.

HARVAR

Thank God.

MICHELLE

What's the matter with the woods?

HARVAR

No fuckin' way. What is it with you people? Your whole family wants me to do that.

TOM Ilesic enters with tools.

MICHELLE

Hello, Mr. Ilesic. Thanks for coming.

TOM

Hello, Michelle. You must be Rune's fella.

HARVAR

I must be. Harvar Blumis.

TOM

Tom Ilesic. Toilet trouble?

MICHELLE

Yes–

HARVAR

Looks like it. I think it's the ballcock? I had a look, but I didn't bring my tools, so…

TOM

I'll get after it.

HARVAR

I wish you would. I'm really looking forward to dropping the kids off at the pool, if you know what I mean.

TOM goes inside. A pause.

MICHELLE
So, do you have to work on Monday?

HARVAR
Hmm? Oh, yes. Or no. I forget. What's on Monday?

MICHELLE
I don't know. Are you guys going back on Monday?

HARVAR
I think we... I forget. Are you?

MICHELLE
No. My first client is on Wednesday.

HARVAR
Oh. That's good.

> *RUNE comes out of the cottage.*

RUNE
She's asleep.

MICHELLE
No, she's not.

RUNE
Yes, she is.

MICHELLE
No, she does this thing where she lets you think she's asleep, and then when you leave, she throws herself onto the floor beside the bed.

RUNE
No, I think she's actually asleep.

MICHELLE
Well, we'll see. If you actually managed to get her to sleep after all the times I tried, I'll fuckin' kill myself.

RUNE
Maybe you should get a nap, too. We'll keep an eye on Lilly.

MICHELLE
Okay. Mr. Ilesic's here.

RUNE
I saw.

MICHELLE
I'll never get to sleep with him banging around, but okay.

RUNE
Okay.

> *MICHELLE goes indoors. RUNE moves away from HARVAR.*

HARVAR
Sweetie?

RUNE
Uh huh.

HARVAR
Everything okay?

RUNE
(She's crying.) Sure.

> *HARVAR goes to her.*

That fucking awful woman.

HARVAR
Which one?

RUNE
God. What must this be like for you? I'm so sorry.

HARVAR
I'm okay.

RUNE
Are you sorry you came?

HARVAR
No.

RUNE
Really?

HARVAR
Look, of course I am, okay? But I'm not gonna say so, so stop asking, okay?

RUNE
Okay. I'm sorry.

HARVAR
I mean, fuck.

RUNE
Sorry.

HARVAR
Sorry.

A pause.

Where are we going, again? On the thing? Your niece asked me and I couldn't tell her. Made me feel like a fucking jerk.

RUNE
Italy. Tuscany.

HARVAR
Don't you think we'd better choose, one or the other? Time's running out.

RUNE
Can we talk about the bachelor party again?

HARVAR
I, fuck, no.

RUNE
Not the content. The timing.

HARVAR
I told you, there's nothing I can do about it. They decided, and they had to figure out everyone's schedule, you know? And, like, we invited your father, and nobody thought he'd come, and then he said yes, but he was out of town and so most of it had to do with fitting in your father.

RUNE
I know.

HARVAR
So, like, talk to your father.

RUNE
I'm actually talking about the timing of the whole thing.

HARVAR
The whole thing?

RUNE
Yes. I don't know, okay? I don't know what I'm saying here. I don't have a thing here I'm trying to talk you into, okay?

HARVAR
Okay.

RUNE

But it just seems that we picked badly. We picked days badly, and times, and everything.

HARVAR

For like, what. The whole thing?

RUNE

Who gets married on a Friday morning?

HARVAR

It was the only time they had.

RUNE

I know, but–

HARVAR

And you needed it to be that week.

RUNE

I know, it's my fault, but–

HARVAR

And I got all those limo's lined up for the Friday.

RUNE

I know, I know, but–. It seems like we made one bad decision early on, and it's forced us to make bad decisions all down the line.

HARVAR

Well, I didn't make them.

RUNE

That's not fair. You have been kept a part of the whole process. All you did was beg to be left out of the decisions, and I wouldn't let you.

HARVAR

Yes, okay.

RUNE

So don't say now that this is all happening without your consent.

HARVAR

Okay, okay.

> *A pause.*

So what are you saying.

RUNE

I'm saying... I don't know.

HARVAR

That we should change everything?

RUNE

I just, I wonder if it would all work better if it got pushed off a couple of weeks. Could we do that? Do you think?

HARVAR

A couple of weeks?

RUNE

We might lose the deposit on the place and everything, but I'm sure my father wouldn't mind.

HARVAR

We'd have to call everybody.

RUNE

Yes. I could do that.

HARVAR

I'd have to see how many cars would be available.

RUNE

Would you mind doing that? That way we could hopefully do it at a better time. It just seems too weird, the way we've been sort of forced into doing it.

HARVAR

Yes.

RUNE

Do you mind doing that?

HARVAR

No.

RUNE

Okay. Good. So…

HARVAR

So, okay.

> *A pause.*

What are we talking about here?

RUNE

Two weeks. Maybe the Saturday the 19th or something.

HARVAR

We're talking about two weeks.

RUNE
Yes. If they can do it.

HARVAR
Are we talking about two weeks?

RUNE
Yes. Of course. Yes. Okay?

HARVAR
Okay.

RUNE
Okay.

A pause.

What.

HARVAR
No. Nothing. I'll do it.

RUNE
Thank you. We'll do all that stuff once we get back to town on Monday, okay?

HARVAR
I don't have to be in on Monday.

RUNE
You don't?

HARVAR
No.

RUNE
Well, I do.

HARVAR
Oh.

RUNE
Okay?

HARVAR
Sure.

RUNE
What, are you dying to stay out here? Just say so.

HARVAR
No, no. We'll go back Monday.

RUNE
> Thank you.

HARVAR
> But what's Michelle going to do with your mother?

RUNE
> She'll figure it out. Mother is her responsibility.

HARVAR
> Okay.

RUNE
> I have to be back to go to work.

HARVAR
> But you work from home. You keep saying you could do your job from anywhere.

RUNE
> I have an editorial meeting. What is this? I thought you'd be thrilled to get away from my family.

HARVAR
> Yeah, okay.

RUNE
> What's going on?

HARVAR
> Did your shrink tell you to put the wedding off?

> *A pause.*

RUNE
> No. And I'm not putting anything off. We're just adjusting it, okay? Okay?

HARVAR
> Okay.

RUNE
> Kiss me. I'm sorry. Kiss me.

> *They kiss. He looks at her.*

HARVAR
> It's okay to be scared. You should be scared. I mean, fuck, look at me. But be scared *with me*, okay? Not by yourself.

RUNE
> I'm not.

HARVAR
You sure?

RUNE
I'm not scared.

HARVAR
If you're not scared, that makes you the stupid one. Ha ha.

RUNE
I'm going to clean up the kitchen. Do you want anything?

HARVAR
No.

RUNE
Do you want a beer?

HARVAR
Maybe later. I'll get it.

RUNE
Okay.

RUNE goes inside. HARVAR takes his shirt off, puts on his sunglasses, and lies down. LILLIAN comes in, dripping wet. She stands over HARVAR, dripping on him. She has a wriggling sunfish in her hands.

HARVAR
That better be water coming off you.

LILLIAN
It is. Look.

HARVAR sits up.

HARVAR
What is that, like a fish?

LILLIAN
No, it's a dump truck, stupid.

HARVAR
Where did you get that?

LILLIAN
I caught it with my hands.

HARVAR
You caught that? barehanded?

A pause while they look at the fish.

LILLIAN
Do you know, my mother won't tell me who my father is?

HARVAR
Really.

LILLIAN
She says it's none of my business.

HARVAR
Well, she's probably got a point there.

A pause. The fish stops wriggling. LILLIAN holds it by the tail.

LILLIAN
Want it?

HARVAR
Um, no thanks.

LILLIAN throws the fish into the bushes.

No, Lilly.

LILLIAN
What.

HARVAR
You can't throw that there.

LILLIAN
Are you telling me what to do? Uncle Harvar?

HARVAR
I, fuck, no. But you leave that there, it'll start stinking. You gotta throw it back in the water or into the woods or something.

LILLIAN
Why.

HARVAR
Because it'll stink. You caught it, you killed it, now it's your responsibility, okay? You got to take responsibility for the stuff you do.

LILLIAN
Okay.

LILLIAN goes to the bushes, starts searching. HARVAR lies down.

You just gonna lie there all day?

HARVAR
> Sweetie, I'm not going to do anything physical until I can get into the bathroom and flash out a loaf.

LILLIAN
> Until what?

HARVAR
> Nothing. I have to poo.

LILLIAN
> You have to poo?

HARVAR
> I have to poo.

> *A pause.*

LILLIAN
> You could poo in the woods.

HARVAR
> I'm not pooing in the woods.

LILLIAN
> Why not? I did twice yesterday.

HARVAR
> Because you may not know this, but when you poo in the woods there's a very strong chance of some *thing* crawling up your ass.

LILLIAN
> That's not true.

HARVAR
> Yes it is.

LILLIAN
> Don't be ridiculous.

HARVAR
> I'm not.

LILLIAN
> Yes, you are. Just like Aunt Rune said. She said you were ridiculous.

> *HARVAR sits up.*

HARVAR
> She did? When did she say this?

LILLIAN
I don't know. She said you were ridiculous, but that there was nothing she could do. She was taking a huge chance getting married to you.

HARVAR
I see. Okay.

LILLIAN
You were the best that she could hope for.

HARVAR
Uh huh.

LILLIAN
And *immatoor*.

HARVAR
Uh huh.

LILLIAN
Does she mean immature?

HARVAR
I guess.

LILLIAN
I get that all the time. Come swimming.

HARVAR
No thanks. I'm gonna… I'm gonna go for a walk.

LILLIAN
Chickenshit.

HARVAR
That's right.

LILLIAN
Ridiculous.

HARVAR
Right. See you later.

> *HARVAR goes. LILLIAN finds the fish, and as she does so, the door bangs open and FRANCES makes her way onto the porch. FRANCES sits. She is breathing hard. She and LILLIAN lock eyes for a moment, then LILLIAN walks toward the cottage. LILLIAN pulls back the lattice that covers the crawlspace, and throws the fish under the cottage. Then she walks off, toward the water. FRANCES touches her blouse, smoothing it with her hand. She*

> *repeats this gesture, until it becomes frantic. She tears open her*
> *blouse and sits back, her hand fluttering over her eyes. TOM exits*
> *the cottage, sees FRANCES, and sits beside her.*

TOM

(He's fixing her clothing, he will eventually take her hand.) Here you
are. I wondered where you were.

Toilet's fixed for now. The seal's going to go on it soon. When that
happens, I might as well replace the whole thing. Toilets are so cheap
these days.

Were you having a rest? Did you eat yet? Michelle make you
something?

Did I tell you, I got down to Toronto a few weeks ago? Maybe I did.
Took myself to a few movies, that kind of thing. I called you, I think
I told you. Did Michelle tell you I called? She couldn't manage to
work out a time for me to come and see you, but I hope she told you
I called while I was in town.

Oh. I sold the business to Tom Junior last week. Did I tell you?
Signed everything last week. It's all his. And now I work part time
for him. Isn't that hilarious? He'll be fine, I think. There's lots lined
up for the fall, two or three houses, and he said he wanted to hire
a full-time bookkeeper, and that sort of thing. So he's got plans.
I guess if he can keep his head out of his ass and his ass out of the
drunk tank, he'll be okay. I guess. I hope. But what the hell. It sure
was odd, sitting in the lawyer's office, my son already had a couple
of beers in him, I'm sure, listening to the guy, our lawyer, just calmly
take my business and hand it over, like a, a, I don't know. Like it was
nothing. Like it wasn't in fact forty-eight years of my life. Thomas
Junior didn't even take his sunglasses off.

I made a flan last week, do you know what that is? I didn't. It's pretty
much a flat pie with no, you know, lid. I had all these strawberries,
I'll sometimes go to Hutchison's and pick them, and I'll sort of
forget myself and look up and I've picked way more than I need.
You ever do that?

So I found the recipe in a cookbook Shelagh left behind, and it took
forever to do, but I figured it would take as long as it takes, just like
when you build anything, you know? And it pretty much did. Crust
took me three tries.

I don't know how long that cookbook had been sitting there. First
time I noticed it since she moved out. She moved to her sister's in

Peterborough. You know, I know I wanted to be alone, but I sure as hell can't remember why anymore.

I should have brought you some. I ate almost all of it, though. Watching God knows what. That program with the Black people yelling at each other. Have you ever seen that? I was watching it, and eating this thing, and I laughed once or twice at it, and then I felt embarrassed for laughing? All alone, sitting there, feeling ashamed because I laughed at this program.

You cold? You feel a bit cold. No?

Damn, I should have brought it. I had a letter published in the local paper. Some guy, some nitwit got permission to build this car wash, you know, where you go into the stalls and wash the car yourself? Put money in the thing and the hose squirts water for five minutes, you know? That kind of thing? You ever seen these places? They look just awful.

The lights begin to fade.

And he gets permission to build it right downtown. Right beside the cenotaph, in between it and the fountain, right there where the old city hall was, right on that site. Stupidest goddamned thing you ever saw. I should have brought the letter I wrote.

Frances, I tell you, you have just about the worst view from here of what is just about the prettiest lake. I don't know.

I guess he's gonna have to change the lettering on the trucks, and get new business cards printed up–

Blackout.

Act Three

*The same, fifteen years later. The cottage has slid another foot
and a half to the left, trees now hang low over the roof. Paint
has continued to degrade, and now weeds push up between the
floorboards of the porch. Early morning. MICHELLE and TOM
JR. are seated on the porch, in the same configuration as their
parents at the end of the previous act. MICHELLE is in pyjamas.
TOM JR. has a beer between his knees, and is looking at some pills
in his hand. Through the following, he will choose one of the pills,
swallow it with some beer, and put the remaining pills in a shirt
pocket.*

MICHELLE
...and the stop light is coming up, and we're just going faster and
faster, and now, the kids in the back seat are screaming, and this girl,
and I know this girl, right? She has a reputation already, this girl,
sixteen years old, and the other ones talk about her like she's filth.
So I have a soft spot for this girl, more or less, I mean, I know where
she is at that moment, that moment in her life, boys and her parents
and all the judgment and hatred at school; I mean, how does anyone
get anything done at all between the ages of thirteen and eighteen?

TOM JR.
I know.

MICHELLE
Honestly. So there we are, screaming towards the red light,
accelerating, I'm standing on my brakes, even though I know
they're disconnected, temporarily disconnected, but still, at that
moment of course it matters little how temporarily, and I grow
calmer and calmer as the noise in the car grows and grows.
Calmer and calmer. I think whole, complete sentences, I plan
for a few different scenarios, post-crash scenarios, I have time to
do this. And then–

TOM JR.
And then you sail through the intersection.

MICHELLE
That's right.

TOM JR.
Everyone was okay.

MICHELLE
That's right.

TOM JR.
Except when the girl finally pulled over, she sideswiped a parked car.

MICHELLE
I've told you this?

TOM JR.
Let's go into the woods.

A pause. Of the view:

MICHELLE
Isn't it awful here.

TOM JR.
You know, the rest of the lake's not bad. This is just like, an ugly spot.

MICHELLE
Did you ever swim here? Before?

TOM JR.
Sure. You and I swam a bunch of times.

MICHELLE
It was awful.

TOM JR.
Back when you let me come over to swim and *et cetera*.

MICHELLE
We used to have to wear old shoes to go swimming, to keep the leeches off, and also because the stones were so sharp.

TOM JR.
That's right.

MICHELLE
Until finally Rune got sick of it and hired someone to dredge out the whole bay.

TOM JR.
Yeah, Michelle. That was me.

MICHELLE
Was it? And then she had all that sand trucked in. She tried to make
a little beach. And it didn't work. The next spring, we came back and
the sand was gone, the rocks were back, and now there were weeds
so thick that you couldn't see the bottom. And, also, part of our
shoreline fell off and disappeared.

TOM JR.
That'll happen.

MICHELLE
And then Rune gave up. What was that?

TOM JR.
What was what?

MICHELLE
What was that you just took?

TOM JR.
Oh. Not sure. I think it was like a muscle relaxant, from when
Tammy hurt her back. Want one?

MICHELLE
No thank you. I'm always curious to see what people are taking. Your
father built this porch.

TOM JR.
I helped him.

MICHELLE
Oh, no. You couldn't have. It was years ago.

TOM JR.
I was little.

MICHELLE
Oh, no. You couldn't have.

TOM JR.
I did.

MICHELLE
No you didn't. My mother could never figure out why he stopped.
She asked him to build a screened-in porch. He built the porch, but
never screened it in. My mother was too embarrassed to ask him to
finish.

TOM JR.
Well, my father, and this won't come as a big surprise, spent most of
his time screwing the townies on their renovations. He'd start a job,

start the next one before finishing the last one, never get around to
doing any of them all the way. People always paid. Jesus, people
loved him. The more he'd screw them, the more people loved him.

MICHELLE

People were at his mercy. And he always pretended they weren't.
That's why people liked your father.

TOM JR.

I deal honestly with people, you know, for the most part, and they
hate me. All they want to talk about is what a guy my father was.

MICHELLE

Can you see Lilly? I can't see Lilly.

TOM JR.

I have four guys working under me. I have a girl that does the books.
I actually pay taxes, for fuck's sake. He till the day he died told me I'd
ruin the business. His business.

MICHELLE

You pay taxes?

TOM JR.

Yes.

MICHELLE

I've never paid taxes on my business.

TOM JR.

Well, see, there you go.

MICHELLE

As far as they're concerned, I've never made a dime. Do you see
Lilly?

TOM JR.

No. Let's go into the woods.

MICHELLE

No. I… I don't do that anymore.

TOM JR.

You don't do that anymore?

MICHELLE

No.

TOM JR.

Since yesterday?

MICHELLE
Oh. Was that you?

TOM JR.
What do you mean, was that me?

MICHELLE
Damn it. Okay then. Soon.

TOM JR.
Who else do you take into the woods?

A pause.

Michelle?

MICHELLE
Nobody.

TOM JR.
Are you sure?

MICHELLE
I… yes. I just thought that maybe I just thought I was in the woods having sex with someone, yesterday.

TOM JR.
No. That was a real event. That's why I'm back.

MICHELLE
Okay. I did wonder, why, if it happened only in my head, was the sex so bad. If it was a real event, that explains it. Okay. We'll go, soon, but you have to promise the sex will be better.

TOM JR.
I can do that. Well, I can promise that.

MICHELLE
Okay. When did she leave, do you remember?

TOM JR.
Who.

MICHELLE
Lilly. She went for a swim across the lake.

TOM JR.
Lilly's here?

MICHELLE
No, that's what I'm saying, she's in the lake.

TOM JR.
I didn't know Lilly was up.

MICHELLE
Of course she is.

TOM JR.
I didn't see her yesterday.

MICHELLE
Of course she's here. I told her she had to come with me.

TOM JR.
Doesn't she live in like England, or something?

MICHELLE
She did.

TOM JR.
But not any more?

MICHELLE
That's right. I asked her to come home.

TOM JR.
Uh huh.

MICHELLE
I don't trust her. At that distance.

TOM JR.
So, Lilly's here.

MICHELLE
She's in the lake. She likes to swim the lake. You had sex with her, did you not?

TOM JR.
What? No. I didn't even know she was here.

MICHELLE
When she was still in high school.

TOM JR.
Of course not.

MICHELLE
I'm sure it was her fault.

TOM JR.
Look, I don't know what she told you, but we never had sex. I never had sex with your daughter.

MICHELLE
I'm sure she did it. You're just lucky she didn't swallow you whole.

TOM JR.
I, look, I–

MICHELLE
Junior. It's okay. She did it, not you. We'll go into the woods soon. When she gets back. Do you want another beer?

TOM JR.
No. Not yet.

MICHELLE
Okay then.

>   *A pause.*

I'm just, I'm stalling, right?

TOM JR.
Sure.

>   *A pause.*

What's your sister's problem?

MICHELLE
Rune? Rune has no problems. What do you mean? She's fine. She's a difficult person, but.

TOM JR.
She treats me like I'm snot or something.

MICHELLE
Oh, well, yes, she detests you. But I don't think she considers that a problem.

TOM JR.
Why? What did I do?

MICHELLE
Well, she's pretty hard on people in general. And, well, you're from the country.

TOM JR.
That's nice.

MICHELLE
And also, she's very protective of me. I'm all she has, more or less.

TOM JR.
Still, it's no reason to be such a bitch.

MICHELLE
It's actually a pretty good one, Junior.

TOM JR.
Please don't call me that.

MICHELLE
I know. Still stalling.

    A pause.

How's your wife? What's her name?

TOM JR.
I don't want to talk about her. I told you that.

MICHELLE
But what's her name?

TOM JR.
Tammy.

MICHELLE
That's right. It's not really appropriate for a middle-aged woman, is it? Tammy? Do you suppose her parents assumed she'd never reach middle age?

TOM JR.
You said that before.

MICHELLE
I'm allowed to repeat myself. I'm allowed to repeat myself. I'm allowed to repeat myself.

TOM JR.
Okay.

MICHELLE
I'm allowed to repeat myself.

    A pause.

Did I ever tell you the story of how my parents found this place?

TOM JR.
Yes.

MICHELLE
Did I?

TOM JR.
Yes.

MICHELLE
Ah.

A pause.

They were in a canoe, from that place across the way—

TOM JR. stands.

TOM JR.
I'm gonna go.

MICHELLE
Don't go, Junior. You don't have to listen.

TOM JR.
Yeah. But. You don't seem… into this whole idea, like you were yesterday.

MICHELLE
I'm just, I'm nervous, okay? Lilly came back.

TOM JR.
Maybe you just need some time to yourself.

MICHELLE
I'd, God, I'd love some time to myself. Between Rune and this one, Lillian, and everything, I can't get a minute to myself.

TOM JR.
Michelle.

MICHELLE
Junior?

TOM JR.
Lilly's not here.

MICHELLE
Yes she is.

TOM JR.
No. Michelle. Lilly's not here.

MICHELLE
She's swimming.

TOM JR.
No, she's not. God.

MICHELLE
She's not?

TOM JR.
See ya later, Michelle.

MICHELLE
Wait! Did you fix the thing?

TOM JR.
I told you. I need a part. I'll be back on Monday. See ya.

MICHELLE
Of course.

> *TOM JR. exits. A pause. MICHELLE stands, peering out into the lake.*

HEY!! HEY!!

RUNE
(from inside; startled awake) What? What is it?

MICHELLE
GET BACK HERE!!

RUNE
What is it? Michelle? What time is it?

MICHELLE
HEY!!

> *RUNE comes outside. She's wearing pyjamas.*

RUNE
Stop shouting. What are you yelling for?

MICHELLE
Lillian's got away again.

RUNE
What?

MICHELLE
She's too far out.

RUNE
Michelle. Goddamn it.

MICHELLE
I can't see her.

RUNE
Lillian's not here.

MICHELLE
Yes she is.

RUNE
Michelle.

MICHELLE
Yes she is. She came last night. She came in the middle of the night.

RUNE
Lillian moved away, remember?

MICHELLE
I know that. Jesus. I know that. Never mind. I'm going out in the canoe.

RUNE
Let me come with you. Something will happen.

MICHELLE
I'm just going out in the canoe. You stay here.

RUNE
Michelle. Something always happens.

MICHELLE
No.

RUNE
Are you sure?

MICHELLE
Yes. Of course. I would do this, anyway, even if you weren't here.

RUNE
Don't go far.

MICHELLE
No. I know what you must think of me.

RUNE
Oh, Jesus. I do not.

> *MICHELLE exits toward the water. RUNE watches her go. She turns to go inside and stops to examine the face of the cottage. She picks at the paint, absently pulls up a weed or two. She turns to watch MICHELLE again. She goes inside. A pause. MATTHEW, now 48, walks on, looks around, and eventually sits. RUNE comes out of the cottage with toast and a spatula.*

MATTHEW
Hey. Hi.

RUNE stops.

RUNE
Hi.

Hello.

MATTHEW
Hello.

RUNE
Well… shit. Hi.

MATTHEW
Nice to see you, Rune. I'm not… it's not too early, is it?

RUNE
Nice to see you. What are you doing here? I mean, Holy shit.

They hug.

MATTHEW
I was at a friend's cottage, and we drove past here on the way up.
I thought of you. I wondered if you still had this place.

RUNE
I know. I can't believe it either. We all hate it so much. Bloodsuckers
get bigger every year.

MATTHEW
It's nice here.

RUNE
It really isn't. So. You're here. Are you here? In Toronto?

MATTHEW
Yes. I moved back in April.

RUNE
From?

MATTHEW
Calgary.

RUNE
That's right. I don't blame you for returning.

A pause.

I'm sorry. I'm a terrible snob.

MATTHEW
Yes. But I knew that already, from the newspaper.

A beat.

No, you're right. Calgary's the kind of place you wind up if you're not paying attention.

RUNE
You're in produce, is that right? Is that what I heard?

MATTHEW
Well, yes. More or less. I was a lawyer for an egg company for a bunch of years. Then I was a lawyer for the wheat board. Then I took some time off. Now, I work with the federal government for some potato people. I'm a potato lobbyist.

RUNE
Wow. All things I can no longer eat.

MATTHEW
And you're doing well. I read you all the time.

RUNE
Thanks.

MATTHEW
Sometimes I even agree with you.

RUNE
Well, thanks.

MATTHEW
Actually, I'm just being polite. I never agree with you.

RUNE
Thank God. I have no respect for people that have any respect for what I write.

MATTHEW
But you're entertaining.

RUNE
That's exactly right. You got married, no?

MATTHEW
I did. I was married for about ten years.

RUNE
I'm amazed and thrilled you had the courage to ask someone else after I turned you down so brutally.

MATTHEW
Well. I found somebody who made it pretty clear she wouldn't say no. And you?

RUNE
No, I never did.

MATTHEW
Really.

RUNE
No. I just shot them down, one after another. You were the first in a long string of brutalised suitors. The beaches were strewn with the lifeless corpses of the men whose hopes and dreams I enflamed and then destroyed.

MATTHEW
Really.

RUNE
No. I'm just being... a complete asshole. It's nice to see you. Do you want some coffee or anything?

MATTHEW
Oh, no thanks. I'm off coffee.

RUNE
You?

MATTHEW
Yeah, well, it gave me colon cancer a few years back, so...

RUNE
Oh. Well, for fuck's sake.

MATTHEW
Yeah. That's what I said.

RUNE
And how are you now? You look well.

MATTHEW
Oh, I am. I beat it, to everyone's surprise. I'd love a glass of water.

RUNE
Of course. Just a sec. Will you hold these?

> *RUNE hands him the toast and the spatula, and goes into the cottage. MATTHEW looks down toward the lake. RUNE returns with water, and they exchange props.*

MATTHEW
Thanks.

RUNE
Sure. Listen. I have to confess something.

MATTHEW
Okay.

RUNE
I can't remember your name.

MATTHEW
Really.

RUNE
I know exactly who you are, but I just, I'm so fuckin' awful with names. It's a curse. I'm so sorry.

MATTHEW
Well, Rune, that's a bit of a blow.

RUNE
It's the kind of thing, that, if we manage to have an entire conversation without you finding out I don't know, then you leave, I remember your name the second you're out of sight.

MATTHEW
Really.

RUNE
Yes. Except now, instead of putting myself through the agony of all of that, I just admit it and get it over with.

MATTHEW
I see. That sounds much healthier.

RUNE
So…

MATTHEW
Much more grown up.

A pause.

RUNE
Are you going to tell me?

MATTHEW
Well, Rune, I don't know.

RUNE
Look you bastard, I said I'm sorry, just remind me what–

MATTHEW
Matthew Grant.

RUNE

(almost simultaneous with the above line) Matthew fuckin' Grant.
Sorry. Sorry.

MATTHEW

I was the guy, '94, I proposed–

RUNE

Yes, yes, I know–

MATTHEW

Offered to take you away from all this–

RUNE

No, I know.

MATTHEW

You described me at the time as the love of your life–

RUNE

I know who you are. And I never called you that.

MATTHEW

Well, it was something like that.

RUNE

Was it?

MATTHEW

Something like that. I recall it quite clearly.

RUNE

Well, what was I, 18 or something?

MATTHEW

You were nearly 21.

RUNE

So.

A pause.

MATTHEW

Don't remember much about the actual proposal. I do remember
driving back to the city the next day, with you, and that was fun.
Very long drive; very, very uncomfortable.

RUNE

Yes. I can remember… seeing the road rush by between my feet.
It was an old car.

MATTHEW

That's right.

RUNE

Whole chunks of it were missing.

MATTHEW

That's right. And I think you got out before the car had actually stopped.

A pause.

How's your mom?

RUNE

She died.

A pause.

MATTHEW

It was the smart thing to do, turning me down.

RUNE

I was just standing here wondering if that was the wrong thing to do.

MATTHEW

Oh, no, absolutely. It was, I was... I had no idea what I was doing.

RUNE

Yes.

MATTHEW

Plus, you would have wound up in Calgary.

RUNE

That's right. Oh, God.

MATTHEW

But it's funny. I feel in a lot of ways like it was the last deliberate thing I ever did. I agonised, I decided, I did it, it didn't work out, and in a funny way, it's like everything since then has been sort of accidental.

A pause.

Or maybe I'm just romanticising it. Maybe I've never done anything deliberate.

RUNE

Maybe.

MATTHEW

Maybe I've gotten through all this time without a single deliberate act. I feel as though I was born without any guiding principles, any instincts. Of any kind.

RUNE

Yes. My mother used to complain of having no instincts.

MATTHEW

Well, she was right to complain. It would be great, don't you think, to actually have strong, ingrained feelings about the things you're confronted with, day after day? To have some sort of system down deep, organising you and making you do things spontaneously, with certainty and in the knowledge that right or wrong, at least you're acting with some sort of integrity.

RUNE

You've given this some thought.

MATTHEW

So have you. I can read it in your column.

A pause.

Or maybe I'm reading that into it.

RUNE

No. I don't think so.

MATTHEW

Anyway. Sorry. Hi.

RUNE

Yes. Hi. Don't apologise. You're absolutely right. Instincts would be useful.

A pause.

MATTHEW

So, apart from the column, what have you been up to?

RUNE

Oh, you know, this and that.

A pause.

Nothing.

A pause.

MATTHEW

What's the spatula for?

RUNE

Hmm? Oh. I had just this minute decided I was going to scrape off the old paint.

MATTHEW

I see.

RUNE

And then probably repaint. That was the idea. My mother would be mortified by the state of the place. I suddenly thought.

MATTHEW

Right.

RUNE

I was asleep, I woke up, I thought of my mother. And then you appeared.

A pause.

MATTHEW

You look well. I should have said that before.

RUNE

Thanks. It's okay.

MATTHEW

How's the paramenopause working out?

RUNE

You can see it, can you? It's that obvious?

MATTHEW

You wrote a column about it.

RUNE

Oh, fuck, yes. That's right. I'm so desperate for ideas from one week to the next that–

MATTHEW

I liked that column. I don't know who wrote it, but it was not written by the person that usually writes your column.

RUNE

I know, I tried to get it back after I submitted it. I felt ridiculous afterward.

MATTHEW

It was good. It was a nice break from all the…

RUNE

Yes?

MATTHEW
Well, bile, I was going to say.

RUNE
Yes.

A beat.

I figured out something early. If you're going to write about society, you'll seem much more interesting if you do one thing: blame the wrong person. If there's a victim, blame the victim. If someone is at a disadvantage, if someone is misinformed, if someone you know to be virtuous shows bad judgment, attack them.

MATTHEW
I see.

RUNE
I mean, newspapers are crammed with writers sticking up for these people.

MATTHEW
Yes.

RUNE
So I provide balance, by appealing to everyone's worst feelings. It's my one true talent.

MATTHEW
I find that hard to believe.

RUNE
Oh, yes it is. I'm an awful person. It's second nature now.

A pause.

Anyway. Can you, do you want to stay for lunch?

MATTHEW
Listen, do you want to get married?

A pause.

During the half a year when I seriously thought I was dying, all I thought about was you.

A pause.

How's Michelle?

RUNE
She's fine. She sort of took over up here when mother died. She wouldn't let me sell it.

MATTHEW

Does she still work in restaurants?

RUNE

Michelle never worked in restaurants.

MATTHEW

She didn't? Wasn't she a chef somewhere? Or training to be a chef?

RUNE

No.

MATTHEW

That's funny. I always thought she was a chef.

RUNE

No. She has a small business she runs when she feels like it.

MATTHEW

Ah. Doing what?

RUNE

Teaching kids to drive.

MATTHEW

Really.

RUNE

I know.

A pause.

MATTHEW

Listen. I'm a very stupid man. I've drifted through much of my life, barely attached to things, to people, without really participating in anything. And I don't expect that to change. I'm forty-eight. I'm, this is it. I don't know anything. I mean that. I don't know what happened to me, I don't know where all my time went, I don't know why I didn't die, I don't know why I'm here. I'm incapable of understanding my own motives. And I think I can safely say at this point in my life that those are things that aren't going to change. So there you go: I'm offering you very little, and I have no real understanding of why I'm doing it. And I'm under no illusions about suddenly becoming a person who believes in things, does things, or understands why he does them.

RUNE

Well when you put it like that, how could a girl resist.

A pause.

You know, I actually do understand my motives. I spent years working at it, figuring it out. With a variety of professionals. I know why I do the things I do. But Mark?

MATTHEW

Matthew?

RUNE

Fuck. Matthew? The thing I've found out is that knowing why you do things doesn't change a motherfucking thing. It doesn't help.

MATTHEW

Well, that's good to know–

RUNE

It's fun, right? It's a great distraction, uncovering the mysteries of your own behaviour. It kills time while you continue to do exactly the same things you've done over and over, all your life. It can even provide the illusion of change, for a while. But eventually, you return to the person you always were, held back by the things that always did, making the same bad decisions you always made. So, what I'm saying is, don't bother. Don't bother trying to figure out why you are the ridiculous way you are, because it doesn't help.

MATTHEW

That sounds pretty… hopeless.

RUNE

I suppose. And yet, I'm not.

MATTHEW

Hopeless?

RUNE

Yes. I'm not.

MATTHEW

Well, so, that's good.

RUNE

Yes. I'm really not, I don't think. No.

A pause.

MATTHEW

So, about the other thing…

RUNE

Yes. Oh. Oh. I really don't think it's a good idea.

MATTHEW
Yes, but–

RUNE
You see–

MATTHEW
I didn't ask what you thought of it as an idea. I asked if you wanted to do it.

A pause.

RUNE
Yes.

MATTHEW
Really.

RUNE nods.

Really?

RUNE
Sure.

MATTHEW
Well, Holy crap. All right. Thanks.

RUNE
Sure.

MATTHEW
Way to go.

RUNE
Way to go.

A pause.

I want you to know, I'm terrible at this.

MATTHEW
Yeah. Well. Look who you're talking to.

RUNE
And I really thought I was done with this stuff.

MATTHEW
Yes.

RUNE
So, please.

MATTHEW
> Please what.

RUNE
> Just, please. I'm going to be terrible at… I'm, I don't know how to…

MATTHEW
> That's funny.

RUNE
> What.

MATTHEW
> I seem to remember you behaving more or less this way when you were turning me down.

RUNE
> Really?

MATTHEW
> Pretty much.

> *A pause. From the water, MICHELLE yells: "Rune!"*

RUNE
> Oh, shit. Sorry. That's Michelle. *(to the lake)* WHAT! STOP YELLING!

MATTHEW
> Is that Michelle?

MICHELLE
> I can't paddle anymore!

MATTHEW
> Oh.

RUNE
> WHY NOT!

MICHELLE
> I just can't! Come out here and get me!

RUNE
> YOU MUST BE KIDDING!

MICHELLE
> I dropped the paddle!

RUNE
> YOU WHAT!?

MICHELLE
You heard me! Get out here!

RUNE pulls off her pyjamas. She's wearing a bathing suit underneath.

RUNE
Sorry about this. You remember Michelle. I'm afraid she's about the same as the last time you saw her.

MATTHEW
Really.

RUNE
More or less. Anyway. I wanted a swim this morning. I'll be back in a couple of minutes. Hand me those shoes?

MATTHEW hands her the beat-up sneakers at his feet.

Honest to God. I could kill her. I could always kill her. I'll be right back. Make yourself at home. Eat that toast.

MATTHEW
Okay. Listen, can I, I have to tell you some–

RUNE
You'll be here when I get back?

MATTHEW
Yes. Yes I will.

RUNE
Well, good.

RUNE goes. She returns, and kisses MATTHEW.

MATTHEW
Hi, Rune.

RUNE
Yes. Hi.

MATTHEW
Matthew.

RUNE
That's right. I…

MATTHEW
Yes?

RUNE

I was thinking about the paint, and my mother, and there you were. I have a hard time believing this… just happened.

MATTHEW

Me too.

RUNE

But it did, right?

MATTHEW

Yes.

RUNE

Yes. It was a real event. Hang on, okay?

MATTHEW

Yes.

RUNE

Okay.

> *She leaves again. MATTHEW watches her. He looks away. RUNE re-enters, stops, and looks at him a long time. Finally, he turns around and sees her. Then she exits again.*
>
> *There is a splash. MATTHEW eats toast. He finishes the water. He goes inside the cottage. A pause. LILLIAN, 25, walks on in a bathing suit. She goes around the cottage, removes the bathing suit, and wraps herself in a towel. MATTHEW comes out onto the porch, drinking a second glass of water. LILLIAN comes around the corner.*

MATTHEW

Oh! Hi!

LILLIAN

Hello.

MATTHEW

Matthew Grant. I didn't realise anyone else was…

LILLIAN

I got here last night. Lillian.

MATTHEW

Hi.

LILLIAN

Hi.

MATTHEW
I'm a friend of Rune's.

LILLIAN
Rune has friends?

MATTHEW
Oh. Uh, I don't know, actually. But I, uh, I guess I'm an old friend of hers.

A pause.

Sorry. Don't let me monopolise you. You must want to, uh…

MATTHEW moves away from the cottage door.

LILLIAN
What.

MATTHEW
Well, get dressed.

LILLIAN
(She doesn't move.) I'm okay. I was swimming. I got tired, so I got out of the lake and walked back. Most people don't know enough to get out when they're tired.

MATTHEW
No.

LILLIAN
You knew Rune back in the old days.

MATTHEW
I guess so. University.

LILLIAN
Old boyfriend.

MATTHEW
I guess so, yes.

LILLIAN
I see. Did you bring a suit?

A beat.

MATTHEW
Oh, no. I didn't really know I was coming.

LILLIAN
You got here by accident?

MATTHEW
Well…

LILLIAN
That's a helluvan accident.

MATTHEW
Ha ha.

> *A pause.*

How's the water?

LILLIAN
Are you staying for lunch?

MATTHEW
I am, I think.

LILLIAN
Fantastic.

MATTHEW
Yes it is.

LILLIAN
It's great for Rune to have company. Even company from the past.

MATTHEW
Is it?

LILLIAN
It really, really is. She's unspeakably lonely.

MATTHEW
Well, so, good then.

LILLIAN
Rune's a difficult… person.

> *A pause.*

What do you do, Matthew? Mind if I guess?

MATTHEW
No. Although I don't think–

LILLIAN
Quiet.

> *LILLIAN takes a couple of steps toward him, looks at him very intently.*

Do you, in the course of your daily routine, do you deal at all with paper?

MATTHEW
With, sorry?

LILLIAN
With... papers?

MATTHEW
Well, yes.

LILLIAN
Hmm. Let me see your hands.

> *MATTHEW holds out his hands. She takes them and feels the palms.*

They feel like... are you in shoes?

MATTHEW
Shoes?

LILLIAN
Are you in shoes of any kind?

MATTHEW
No. Potatoes.

LILLIAN
Really? A shoe buyer? A shoe salesman? Can you size me?

> *She offers her foot, losing her balance a little. He grabs her foot to steady her.*

MATTHEW
Oops.

LILLIAN
Oops.

MATTHEW
Uh...

LILLIAN
What size is that?

MATTHEW
Uh... Oh Jesus.

> *He drops her foot.*

LILLIAN
What is it?

MATTHEW
I think you've got a…

LILLIAN
(feeling the underside of her foot) A leech? Ah, yes. There she is. Tucked up in my extraordinarily high arch.

MATTHEW
Yes. Is there any…

He sees a box of salt. Handing it to her:

Here you go.

LILLIAN
Can you get it? Here. Sit down.

He sits. She sits on the ground, and puts her foot in his lap. He pours the salt on the leech. LILLIAN's towel falls open, and were she to open her legs even slightly, he would see everything, as it were.

MATTHEW
Hold still.

LILLIAN
Yes.

They're frozen as the salt does its stuff.

MATTHEW
I'll just. Put some more on.

LILLIAN
Yes.

Some spills on her leg. She wipes it away.

MATTHEW
Sorry.

A pause.

LILLIAN
Can you pull it off?

MATTHEW
No. I can't.

She removes her foot from his lap, crosses it over the other leg. She removes the leech. She stands before him.

LILLIAN
Thank you.

She opens the towel and, facing him, sits on his lap.

Thank you.

MATTHEW
No, listen—

LILLIAN
No.

She kisses him. MICHELLE enters.

MICHELLE
Lillian!

LILLIAN
Go away, mother.

RUNE enters.

MICHELLE
Junior?

MATTHEW
No.

RUNE
What's happening?

MATTHEW
Please.

MICHELLE
Get off him!

MICHELLE pulls LILLIAN off of MATTHEW.

MATTHEW
Michelle.

MICHELLE
You're not Junior.

MATTHEW
No.

RUNE
Matthew?

MATTHEW
I didn't–

MICHELLE
Who the fuck are you? What are you doing to her?

MATTHEW
Matthew–

RUNE
It's Matthew Grant. *(to LILLIAN)* What did you do?

LILLIAN
It was a bloodsucker.

RUNE
(to LILLIAN) What are you doing here?

MICHELLE
It's who? Who are you?

LILLIAN
I got in last night.

MATTHEW
It's Matthew Grant, Michelle. Hello. Sorry. Rune.

RUNE
What.

MICHELLE
Matthew Grant? Matthew Grant?

RUNE
Michelle. Go indoors.

MICHELLE
Matthew Grant. I had sex with Matthew Grant.

RUNE
You what?

MICHELLE
I had sex with you. Didn't I? Were you my lover?

LILLIAN
Oh yes?

MATTHEW
No, I, yes. We–

MICHELLE
When was this?

RUNE
When was this?

MATTHEW
A long time ago.

RUNE
When? Matthew?

LILLIAN
When was this?

MICHELLE
(to LILLIAN) Oh, fuck, oh no. Go indoors!

LILLIAN
I'm not a child.

MICHELLE
Go! Now! Go! Now! Go!

LILLIAN
Stop shouting.

RUNE
When was this?

MATTHEW
It didn't mean anything.

MICHELLE
It didn't mean anything? What you did to me?

MATTHEW
No, Michelle, it didn't. You know that.

MICHELLE
Tell her that!

Meaning LILLIAN. A pause.

LILLIAN
Oh.

Oh yes. I see. That's... funny.

LILLIAN approaches MATTHEW.

Well. Daddy. Hello. That was close.

LILLIAN leans over, and, holding his face, kisses him. She then goes inside.

MATTHEW
   (to RUNE) I... I'm sorry.

MICHELLE
   What are you doing here?

MATTHEW
   I don't know. I just... it was an accident. I came to see Rune.

MICHELLE
   Rune doesn't need that.

MATTHEW
   I'm sorry.

MICHELLE
   We can't have these problems. She can't do it. She's not set up to have things like this. Rune can't handle things like this. She doesn't need you. She's with me. You have to go.

MATTHEW
   Rune?

RUNE
   What.

   MATTHEW can't find a thing to say to her. MICHELLE abruptly charges for him. She hits him and clutches at him.

MATTHEW
   Michelle.

MICHELLE
   You can't come here. You can't come here.

MATTHEW
   I'm sorry.

   MATTHEW has broken free.

   Okay.

MICHELLE
   You–

MATTHEW
   No, okay. Okay.

   MATTHEW leaves.

MICHELLE
   He can't do that. Not now. Rune? You don't want that.

RUNE
Michelle. It's okay.

MICHELLE
Why was he here? Why was he here?

RUNE
I don't know. It's okay, Michelle. You're okay.

MICHELLE
He left us. He can't do that. He can't do that. This is why we shouldn't invite people here.

RUNE
He… wasn't invited.

MICHELLE
That's right. Lillian! Oh God. Lillian!

MICHELLE goes inside.

Lillian! I'm sorry, Lilly. He's a friend of Rune's okay? He came here by himself, okay? And we didn't plan for any of it, for him to be here when you were here.

RUNE walks off. Music begins.

LILLIAN
(crying) Mother. Shut the fuck up.

MICHELLE
What did you say? What did you say to me?

LILLIAN
You deserve all of it. You deserve every awful thing that's ever happened to you.

MICHELLE
What? No I don't. You come back here! Lillian! You come back here!

The music rises and the arguing fades. A long pause with music. The lights change to dusk, then to dawn. It's now sometime in the future. Eventually RUNE enters from the cottage, sits on the porch. She's in pyjamas. The music fades. To herself:

RUNE
Pretty.

A pause.

I hired that man, I spent God knows how much, and they came with a load of sand for our little bay, to make it a more decent swim.

I wanted… to be able to swim without fear, without having to worry. But. It just remains an embarrassment. When people come here, what must they think? Mother used to handle people. Their disappointment. Mother used to handle disappointment. She – what is that smell?

A pause.

There is so little comfort. So little comfort. That when it's offered, you can't… you mustn't hesitate to take it. Just because of where it comes from.

A pause.

I tried to make this a motherfucking project. I did try. *(over her shoulder)* Are you making toast?

A pause.

Darling? Are you making toast?

A pause.

That little criminal. Brought all that sand, took all the stones away. Took our money. A year later it was all gone, and the stones were back. His father never would have. His father would have done a proper job. He liked mother. He liked mother. *(over her shoulder)* Did you? Have a cottage? In Calgary? *(to herself)* Do they have cottages in Calgary? What would be the point? My parents found this place.

MICHELLE enters in pyjamas. She has toast.

MICHELLE
Did you say something?

Rune?

RUNE looks at MICHELLE, confused. She looks back at the cottage. She looks at MICHELLE.

Did you say something?

A pause.

RUNE
No. I didn't say anything. I was just talking.

MICHELLE
Toast? Rune?

Lights slowly fade to black.

MICHELLE
Rune? Rune?

RUNE
I'm okay.

Blackout.

Michael Healey graduated from the Ryerson Theatre School's acting program in 1985. His first play, a solo show called *Kicked*, premiered at the Fringe of Toronto Festival in 1996. It toured nationally and internationally, and won a Dora Mavor Moore Award for best new play in 1997. He is co-author, with Kate Lynch, of *The Road to Hell*, a pair of one-act comedies which premiered at the Tarragon Theatre in 1999. *The Drawer Boy* premiered at Theatre Passe Muraille in 1999, and won the Dora, Chalmers and Governor General's Awards. It has been produced across North America, in Europe and in Australia, and has so far been translated into Japanese, German and French. *Plan B* premiered at the Tarragon Theatre (where he is a playwright-in-residence) in 2001, winning the Dora Award that year.